Wil

from: paula
May 05
Mother's Day

Dufftown

Rural life in Southern Indiana during the Great Depression and World War II

Judge Hugo C. Songer

Guild Press of Indiana, Inc.
Zionsville, Indiana

Library of Congress Number 00-110704

ISBN: 1-57860-090-1

The author, Charlie Songer, on the rumble seat of Harold Helgaman's Ford at Kessner's Bridge.

Table of Contents

Foreword

Duff, a small village situated in a valley on the western edge of Dubois County in southern Indiana, was a special place in time that captivated me as a boy. My memories of Duff and its townspeople have been a constant source of joy throughout my life. Not more than a hundred people called the place home, although the "suburbs," the family farms within a two-mile radius, probably contained another hundred. The time, place, and circumstances fostered a group of people whose shared experiences so bonded them that they continue to communicate with each other, regardless of where life has taken them.

The decades of the 1930s and 40s was the time—decades that included the two defining events of the 20th century: the Great Depression and World War II. It was impossible to escape the effects of those events, no matter where you lived! The place was one of isolation with the nearest town being five miles away—not much of a distance unless you are required to walk, which we often did. Very few people had cars and after spring thaws, those who did frequently got hung up in the middle of dirt roads. During the war years, with gas and tire rationing, our isolation continued for different reasons. The circumstances were that we worked and played only with each other, and the group was small enough that we knew most of the intimate details of each other's lives. Oddly enough, this did not prevent us from being different—we were all characters in our own way.

Before television and mass advertising, in an era when people were still highly individualistic, everyone had complete freedom to develop his or her own unique personality. Conventional thinking often characterizes people of that era as highly conformist and that might have been true of people in *Main Street* as described by Sinclair Lewis, but it definitely did not apply to the people of Duff. There were the highly religious and the atheists, the kindly loving and the grouchy, the contentious and the docile, the fighters and the peace-lovers, the repressed and the sexually liberated. More than that, each had idiosyncrasies that defined his or her uniqueness, neither blended by the melting pot of modern society nor bombarded by messages of mass conformity. The combination of nature and nurture made them who they were, just themselves. No Ipana toothpaste smile, no Marlboro puffing—roll your owns will do nicely; no deodorant or fine perfumes: "Worth makes the man, want of it the fellow. The rest is all but leather and prunella."—Alexander Pope.

I'm not attempting to make them anything they were not. Few were educated or well read—an eighth grade education was the norm. There were the usual hatreds and dislikes, and sometimes their emotions boiled over into violence, even murder. Duff was a microcosm of any society at large, except for anonymity—everyone knew everyone else. Rarely did anyone do anything totally out of character—the typical response to someone's eccentric behavior was "Well, that's what he does," or "That's who she is."

Ever since I grew up there, I have been fascinated by the place and the people. It isn't that I never left. At the outbreak of the Korean War, I enlisted in the army with two other Duff boys. After training I was assigned overseas and spent thirty months in the Far East, near Tokyo, Japan. Discharged in 1954, I spent only a few months at home, and then moved away, never to live in Duff again. After college and law school I practiced law twenty years before finishing my career as a judge, but that did not diminish my enchantment with Duff.

Ethnically, Duffers were, like most Americans, a mixture, although they were exclusively Anglo-Saxon. The earliest settlers, residents of old Dufftown, were Scots—the Osborns, Lemonds, Gambills, Colliers, Collins, Fishers, Spurlocks and the Halls. Their progeny lent a degree of sophistication with an emphasis on literacy. Then came those of English, Welsh and Irish stock: the Stapletons, Peaches, Davises, Joneses, Maxeys, Stilwells, Mayos, McIlrees, and the Smalls, certainly less serious than the Scots and in fact the source of most of the antics on the store porches. Most of the surrounding farms were owned and operated by people of German heritage—the Weisheits,

Bormans, Fennemans, Rauschers, Hilgemans, Hochmeisters, Sundermans, Spitzers, Steinekers, Reinbolds, Hoffmans, and Hopfs. They had an amused and stoic detachment in viewing the antics of the rest of us, all except Ed Ermert, the eccentric German blacksmith who lived between our house and Duff. Nothing detached or stoic about him—he was usually square in the middle of things.

Although I was a full participant in the goings on, part of me was an observer because of my fascination with the characters. To some degree I was standing back and watching, always the enchanted onlooker, which caused me to remember the stories they told and the things they did. Theirs is an interesting story and all my life I have wanted to tell it.

Acknowledgements

I wish to thank friends and family of old Duff, living and dead, who shared the experience of growing up there and told their stories or added details to my own recollections. Some of them are: Gladys Peach, still living in Duff, and my mother Clarissa Songer, both age 97 as I write; Ruth (Jones) Finneman, Harold Hilgeman, Guthrie Sunderman, Leonard "Buck" Borman, Harold "Chalk" Ermert, Charles E. "Gene" Brown, Ralph Lemond, Raymond and Martha (Posey) Stapleton, and Gordon Hochmeister.

My niece, Lorraine Martindale, a freelance editor and writer in New York City, provided helpful advice and comment.

A special thanks go to two people: my wife, Mae and my friend Lloyd (Gobby) Collins. Gobby grew up in Duff ten years ahead of me. He relates several of his own experiences in Duff, and writes so well, I used his own words to tell them. Gobby has his own book-sized collection of stories, some of which date to pioneer times, learned at the knees of his ancestors who added so much to the lore of Duff.

This book, the realization of a long-cherished dream, would not have been possible without the essential help of my wife, Mae Chinn Songer. She has heard these stories for over twenty years, and her encouragement in turning them into a book, her aid in editing, adding phrases which enhanced the meaning of the book, and her typing and proofing of the material are deeply appreciated. She has encouraged and supported me every step of the way from the first word to publication . . . in effect, birthed this book with me, and her contribution is immeasurable.

THE SONGERS

My great-grandmother, Mary Ann (Fisher) Songer, was a resident of Dufftown. Her grandfather, William, was a pioneer settler and a great hunter. She met William Floyd Songer while he was on leave from Company B, of the 42nd Indiana Infantry during the Civil War. They were introduced by Mary Ann's brother William, also of Company B, who was killed at the Battle of Stones River. They married in 1863, and after the war, Mary Ann and Floyd raised nine children in a log house on the original Fisher homestead. My grandfather, James Morgan, was the eldest, born in 1865. I have vivid memories of visiting Grandma Mary Ann with my Dad. Even though times had changed she continued to live the old pioneer way . . . heating the cabin with a fireplace, making thread on a spinning wheel which sat in the corner, and wearing hand-made cotton print dresses that extended to the floor. As was the practice then, she raised most of her food in the garden and saved seed stock from one year to the next. Early one spring, she had made a furrow for a row of peas and dropped them one by one only to learn upon reaching the end of the row, that her old white goose had followed her down the row swallowing the peas. Mary Ann was out of peas, so there was only one thing to do. She killed the goose, retrieved the peas, and finished her planting.

Floyd's behavior was difficult to understand. He was a binge drinker and sometimes disappeared for a week or two. He had a friend, Wyatt Corn, who lived a few miles away in adjoining Pike County, and often when he left home (or the home of one of his children after he and Mary Ann divorced in 1896), it was assumed he was going to visit Wyatt Corn. Everette McIlree and his father Albert were cutting sprouts in one of their fields one day when Floyd walked by. Floyd whooped, "That's the way to do it Albert," and Albert

Mary Ann (Fisher) Songer

replied, nasally, "That's right Floyd." Albert asked, "Where ye goin' Floyd," and Floyd replied, "Well, I reckon I'm jest goin' to the end of the road." After Floyd walked on, Everette, intrigued by Floyd's response, asked Albert, "Dad, where is the end of the road?" And Albert replied, as he watched Floyd disappear around the bend, "Well Son, I reckon it ends at Wyatt Corn's place."

There is no question that Floyd had some terrible experiences in the Civil War. His best friend was killed at Stone's River and Floyd was captured there. Fortunately for him, General Grant, who later pursued a war of attrition and ended the exchange of prisoners, was not yet Commanding General, and Floyd was exchanged after only a couple of months in captivity. At Chickamauga, blood from a friend killed next to him splattered on Floyd's face—it had to be a horrifying, gut-wrenching experience. As an old veteran, he held his niece Emma, my Dad's sister, and sang, "Don't bury me, on Chickamaugee."

Orphaned at age nine, Floyd was the youngest of eight children born to Jacob and Elizabeth (Wilson) Songer. They had left the beautiful Shenandoah Valley in Virginia for free land on the frontier, and upon reaching the Ohio River, loaded their belongings on a flatboat and floated downriver, landing at Troy, Indiana. They entered land next to a creek in a small valley in Spencer County and farmed for a living. (The Lincoln family did the same thing only a few miles away.) After his parents died in 1852, Floyd resided with his older brother Wilson, who also lived in Spencer County and it was from there, in 1862, that Floyd enlisted in the 42nd Regiment. According to his enlistment papers, his father consented, which was highly unlikely, since he had been dead for ten years.

Upon returning home from the Civil War, Floyd farmed for a living. He was a leader in the community and found his voice as a debater in the issues of the day, at meetings in various one-room school buildings in the area. He took the affirmative on the proposition that "Men are totally depraved," and the reporter, tongue firmly in cheek, said:

William Floyd Songer — Civil War Soldier

The debate on total depravity, with Robert A. Bolin and William F. Songer is now at a close. The Christian brethren are responsible for all damages done to the schoolhouse, and so they stopped it.

They were afraid so much talent and eloquence would press the "Gabriel" ends out of the house and it would be hard on them to foot the bill.

He took the affirmative on the resolve that railroads are more useful to man than rivers, but the question was decided in favor of the negative. In 1893 the subject was: "Resolved, that women should have equal rights with men," but again, Floyd lost when it was decided that they should not. He and Elmer Small carried the day at the Duff schoolhouse, when they took the negative on the proposition that "the Negro is no specie of humanity." Apparently Floyd's liberalism came to the attention of the Knights of the Golden Circle, a reactionary organization which was the precursor of the Ku Klux Klan. The newspaper report said:

We are informed that some rascals who probably wanted to throw suspicion off from themselves, visited the house of Floyd Songer in Patoka Township in this county, one night last week, and took him from his bed into the woods, giving him, after a rope was put about his neck, two minutes to prepare for eternity, when they swung him up to a limb. After letting him hang for a short time they took him down, and tried to make him confess that he knew something about the stealing of Mayo's horse a few weeks ago. He protested his innocence when they let him go. These self-constituted detectives had better be careful, or they may get their own precious necks in a halter. Too much anxiety sometimes betrays itself.

The wife of one of the debaters named "Prucilla," although that is undoubtedly a pseudonym, wrote the *Jasper Courier* regarding these debates, and her spunky remarks are proof that women of the time were not exactly shrinking violets, but rather intelligent and amusing. On November 9, 1877, Prucilla wrote "A Cracker's Neck Item"

> *Mr. Editor—As no one has given you any items from this place for some time, I thought I would take the trouble to tell you we have or rather they have–that is the men have organized a debating society, which meets once a week to discuss weighty matters. My husband is the very centre post of the affair and though not a centre post myself, I am tolerably well posted. They have not asked my agreeable company yet, but I blame my husband for that, as I have a habit he doesn't like; of arresting his coattail when he raises up to make a mental shipwreck of himself. The subject of debate last week was, "Is the mind of man superior to that of woman?" My husband says anybody that knowed anything knows man is the smartest. Of course I agree with him. (I never rouse any unnecessary antagonism by disagreeing with him.) I told him I know he would gain any point he undertook and he told me their strongest argument was that Columbus discovered America. Of course, only after a woman equipped him for the voyage, and we all know he would have discove*red *it 70 days sooner if he'd had a smart, capable woman at his elbow. But let 'em argue their side; we can bait them with soft soap and submission, and we get our own way at last, and they will be sure to follow ours. I wrote my man's speech for him to convince the world that men are the smartest. I suppose the sisters generally prepared their husbands and beaux for the occasion; hence the result. The subject for next Friday: "Will a person do more for fear of punishment than reward?"* Prucilla–

And again on November 24, she wrote: "Cracker's Neck Eloquence"

> *Editor Courier;*

Having myself appointed a committee of six to visit the Debating Society and report proceedings, I herewith send you a notice of last Friday night's debate. The Society was called to order by R.A. Bolin. Judges were chosen and a President appointed. R.A. Bolin made a short speech, which was replied to by a tall man with incendiary whiskers and a nose to match, and a windy manner of talking (almost certainly Floyd since we know he debated Bolin). He threatened to lay the question forever at rest; the smallest child in the house should be convinced; hundreds yet unborn should acknowledge, before he was done, that possession is better than pursuit. The house didn't fall, nor the hills bow down, as they should, if I had been bossing them. He told an affecting story about a man getting hung for murder. I didn't observe any tears, but many blew their noses, as if tears were not far off. I don't remember all the speeches, but one had an original idea about the sun pushing up her modest face behind or above the eastern hills. Some made very good speeches; others went out on the floor with ever so many fine ideas and lost them before they got through addressing the President and Judges. After hunting in their pockets, whiskers and hair, they took refuge behind a bad cold, which prevented their saying anything on that occasion. Altogether, the Cracker's Debating Society is a success. The subject for next meeting is as follows: "Resolved, that married life is worse than single life." Prucilla–

Floyd became a preacher in the Primitive Baptist Church and gained a reputation as a real student of the Bible. In 1895 it was reported that Reverend Songer "preached an interesting sermon at the Baptist Church Friday night and everyone went home rejoicing," but in 1897 the Huntingburg paper reported: "Floyd Songer, on the charge of intoxication and swearing in front of women was fined five dollars and costs by Squire Johnson yesterday morning. Failing to pay same, he was taken to jail at Jasper yesterday afternoon." The Primitive Baptist Church had very strong rules against the use of alcohol and excluded him four times. When the world was too much for him, Floyd donned his best suit of clothes, including his white gloves, took all the money he had, and without any warning or explanation, left. In a week or so, he returned, tattered and torn, but somehow refreshed. A man who knew him well said he could always tell when Floyd was about to backslide, because he would be heard singing his favorite hymn, "Greenfields." Some of the verses were as follows:

How tedious and tasteless the hours
When Jesus no longer I see
Sweet prospects, sweet birds and sweet flowers
Have all lost their sweetness to me

The mid-summer sun shines but dim;
The fields strive in vain to look gay;
But when I am happy in him,
December's as pleasant as May.

Dear Lord, if indeed I am thine,
If thou art my sun and my song,
Say, why do I languish and pine,
And why are my winters so long?

Oh drive these dark clouds from my sky
Thy soul-cheering presence restore;
Or take me unto thee on high,
Where winter and clouds are no more.

Whether Floyd experienced a loss of faith and went on a binge, or went on a binge and experienced overwhelming guilt, I do not know. Perhaps Floyd never knew himself. I think it was the war. Post-traumatic stress syndrome had not been thought of, but we wouldn't have any difficulty with that explanation today. His friend, Tennessee

Mary Ann Songer (3rd from l) with three of her children Minie, Tom and James.

Pirtle, who had served in the 58th Regiment drawn from Dubois County and neighboring Pike and Gibson Counties, had even more difficulty readjusting. He got into a fight nearly every time he went to town. Incidentally, Pirtle had great difficulty obtaining a pension. It was not a question of his disability—he was clearly disabled. Many Duffers filed affidavits on his behalf to the effect that he had in fact lived in Duff before the war, he had married a local girl, and Yes—his name was Tennessee Pirtle! The reluctance to grant the pension involved only his having been named after a rebel state, "Tennessee."

My Dad, who was fifteen when his Grandpa died, was very close to Floyd, and had adopted many of his sayings. Sometimes, when I tried to get an exact answer out of him about something, he'd say: "Three in a hill and sometimes a punkin," referring to the time when corn was planted in hills, instead of rows. Three grains of corn were planted in a hill, and sometimes, but not every time, and not even every other time, a pumpkin seed. In other words, there is no exact rule; it's whatever feels right. If Dad found himself in a place he did not want to be, he'd say: "Oss'll tell ye Sonny, this is no place for an old soldier." Years later, when my Dad lay dying on a hospital bed in the corridor of a local hospital, I asked him what Floyd would say if he were in that predicament, and he replied, "Oss'll tell ye sonny, this is no place for an old soldier." Those were the last words I ever heard him say.

My grandpa, James M. Songer, had a more stocky build than Floyd had, dark brown hair and penetrating blue eyes. A well-liked county politician, he made a living with his wits rather than by manual labor. He would buy a farm, live on it a while, and then sell it, hopefully making a profit on the deal. He did the same thing with horses. Grandpa never learned to drive an automobile, so he would hitch a ride from a neighbor, or use the jolt wagon and a team of horses. He, like Floyd, was a drinker and several people told me in later years how Jim Songer had prevailed upon them to give him a ride to Hoffman Brothers farm north of Duff so that he could get some moonshine whiskey, or to Jum Lemond's, for some boot leg whiskey. After

Grandpa drank a little "white lightning," he danced a great jig called the "backstep" which he demonstrated at dances held in homes and granaries around Duff. One hot summer afternoon he was in Charlie Spurlock's store playing checkers with Cecil Smith, who everyone called "The Captain." Lloyd "Gobby" Collins, whose love for Duff is like mine, described the situation this way:

> *Jim had lost two games to the Captain, as the light was bad and he had trouble keeping up with Cap's shifty moves. Suddenly, the door flew open and in came Red Lemond with his mouth harp; Elmer Lemond brought a banjo, Harold Gearner had his fiddle and Fuzz Kays a guitar. They trooped in and stood before the checkerboard and Red began a sic'em speech about the good old days when Jim and his gang was out dancin' and guzzlin' all night, and about all the fun they had, ending on a note that he would bet old Jim could dance the shoes off anybody in town YET. Jim jumped up and shouted, "Yuh dang right I can–hit me a few notes, boys." The band began to play and Jim began a jig dance. The faster they played, the faster Jim danced until the pace reached an unbelievable crescendo. I had not noticed what song they were playing, but suddenly it dawned on me that they were playing, "When the Roll is Called Up Yonder," and not "Over the Waves" or some old square dance number. Jim didn't care–he was just turned on by the music. His furious gyrations came to a sudden halt as he gasped for breath . . . staggered out the door and headed for home. The band stopped playing, laughing in triumph as it realized a mission accomplished. Charley Spurlock (Jim's son-in-law) took a chaw on his plug and unsmilingly shook his head, saying "Danged old fool."*

Jim and several others were loafing on Wayne's store porch one September afternoon when his nephew, Lem Small, began to brag about some home-made peach brandy he had, insisting that it was absolutely the best stuff ever to touch his lips. Lem knew that the brandy was still "green" and caused diarrhea. He carried on about it for awhile, as only Lem could, when finally Jim was convinced that it really must be good stuff, and furthermore, he would like to have some of it. So Lem whipped out the jug and there, in the warmth of a waning September afternoon, Jim took a couple of long swigs and then a couple more. Soon, he began squirming on the porch bench and before long said: "I allow I had better head for the house." Off he went, up the road toward the Songer homestead, just across from Duff School. Halfway to Ed Ermert's blacksmith shop, he began to trot, and soon he broke into a dead run. About a hundred yards from the barnyard gate, he saw the school kids coming down the road, school having been dismissed for the day. He vaulted over the barnyard fence and headed for the nearest stall door. Naturally, the loafers on Wayne's store porch had gone to the middle of the road and gleefully watched him all the way.

Jim didn't hold a grudge over the incident. After all, not only was Lem the son of his sister Ellie, who was married to Elmer Small, but Lem credited Jim with saving his life. One day, Jim and Lem were cutting sprouts when Jim noticed that Lem was spitting blood. Jim suspected T.B., or consumption as it was called, because Archie, Lem's brother, had died of it. Jim enrolled Lem in the Woodmen of the World, a fraternal organization which carried a policy on its members that included coverage for the treatment of certain diseases including T.B. Then he sent Lem to Doc Taylor in neighboring Velpen, who confirmed the diagnosis. Soon, Lem was on his way to a Colorado sanitarium where several months of clean mountain air and "healthy interaction" with the entire nursing staff helped him recover from the disease. Grandpa died when I was four years old, but I remember that he carried me around a lot and brought orange candy slices when he visited and pretended not to have them when I patted his pockets. Once when he was carrying me to a field where Dad was plowing we saw a snake, a blue racer, and Grandpa said "look Sonny, there goes a snik." I remember that he wore a homberg hat, a fitting tribute to his political life, and bib overalls, appropriate for his

Partenheimer Family
Grandmother Katherine Bretz on far right; Charlie Songer, in diapers on far left.

occupation as a farmer.

Jim was a popular man in the community and because he had spent time hanging around the courthouse, knew a little law and was someone to whom Duffers would come for advice. He was always willing to help people, which is what any good politician should do. Jim was a strong Democrat and named his first two sons, both of whom died in infancy, after two nationally known Democratic politicians, William Jennings Bryan and Champ Clark. He loved to argue politics, figuratively listing his arguments in the palm of his left hand with two fingers of his right hand.

Jim married Louise Sunderman, sister of Henry (Andah) Sunderman. By all accounts they had a stormy relationship caused by Jim's drinking and Louise's opposition to it. They raised four children: Minnie, the oldest, married to Charles Spurlock, Duff storekeeper; my Dad, Hugo Elijah; and Emma and Florence. Dad was tall and handsome, and had inherited the piercing blue eyes of his grandfather. He carried himself with considerable dignity–not by design–he was just naturally that way except when he was drinking. He was born at Shakerag, a pioneer settlement located one mile southwest of Duff, so named because a housewife could attract the attention of a neighbor by shaking a rag or hanging it outside on a clothesline. When Dad was six Jim bought the Robert Small farm (out of which Duff had been carved) and the family moved to Duff. It was a working farm, but Grandpa had other priorities, so he and Dad just piddled around on it and Dad never really learned how to farm. During Dad's growing-up years Grandpa Jim was a man of better-than-average means. The family had a Model T, which Grandpa never learned to drive, so one of Dad's few jobs during his teen years was driving his Dad back and forth to the courthouse. His parents never wanted him to leave home for work like the other boys, saying, "Oh Hugo, you've got plenty to do here at home." By Dad's own admission, his mother once bought him a twenty-five dollar silk shirt at a time when you had to work at least two weeks to earn that much money.

Dad's three sisters, especially Emma, doted on him as well, always arranging dates for him, and being critical of girlfriends they hadn't introduced. Then he met my mother, Clarissa Amalia Bretz, a fourth generation German-American girl and after several dates, Grandpa Jim, concerned that their relationship was getting too serious, said, "Hugo, why don't you marry a nice American girl?" making it clear what his real motive was since he was married to a German-American woman himself. He didn't want Dad to get married, period. After Hugo and Clarissa were going steady, Aunt Emma arranged a date for him with another girl, which resulted in Dad's breaking a date he had with Clarissa. Mom found out about it and left for Evansville, a city about fifty miles away, where she hired out to a wealthy family as a cook. It was common at the time for German-American girls to do this because they had high morals, were hard workers, trustworthy, and good cooks. A couple of years passed, during which time Dad realized he had been bitten hard by the love-bug. Through a mutual friend, he arranged a meeting with Clarissa; they started dating again and soon were engaged to be married.

When Dad and Mom married in 1925, Jim and Louise moved out of the Songer homeplace and let the newlyweds move in, but not before placing a mortgage on the farm in order to buy themselves a home in Duff. Actually, there was nothing unfair about that, but the Depression began in a few years and the mortgage became a hard reality with which our family had to contend for a decade. Alex Lemond, who held the mortgage, required only the payment of interest which was a mere eighty-four dollars a year. Putting that sum together every year wasn't easy, but it gave positive structure to our lives during the Great Depression. While many people languished in despair, we had a clear goal and worked towards it every day. Near the end of each year, Dad and Mom sat at the table after we finished eating, tallied the amount set aside to date, and talked about anticipated sources of income, wondering if they would be able to meet the deadline. Cash was extremely hard to come by during the Depression, and I listened to those discussions with considerable anxiety because I hated to think of losing our farm.

It might seem odd to describe my mother, Clarissa Amalia Bretz, with the hyphenated phrase, German-American, when she was in reality a fourth generation American. But since 1837, when her great grandparents immigrated from Volksheim, Hessen-Darmstadt, Germany, not one of her American forebears had married a non-German. In the town where she grew up, appropriately named, Bretzville, everyone continued to speak German and follow their German customs. Bretzville's public school conducted its classes in the German language. Our visits to Mom's relatives usually involved butchering, wheat threshing, corn shredding, or perhaps a family reunion, which included the extended Bretz/Partenheimer families. There was much speaking in the German tongue, joke telling, and drinking homemade wine, even as the work was done. One or two family members, and notably Rob Bretz, a self-taught veterinarian, seemed exempt from work because of their role as family jesters.

Rob sold a lot of lice powder. His practice was to knock on a farmstead door and tell the hausfrau he had lice powder for sale to treat her chicken flock. She might insist that her chickens had no lice, so Rob would ask her to catch a hen and provide a newspaper for a demonstration he was about to make. He suspended the hen over the newspaper, ruffled the feathers, and when harmless chicken lice fell onto the newspaper, Rob had another sale. His job at extended family work enterprises, as far as I could tell, was to go from one group of workers to another, telling jokes and keeping them entertained. After work and dinner, card games began in earnest (usually a game called "sheephead"). Wine-drinking increased in tempo, and fierce arguments over the game or an alleged dumb play, broke out. Voices became louder; there was fist-shaking and name-calling, all in German, as they pounded the table. Based on my past experience in Duff, when voices were raised to that level, all hell was about to break loose and somebody might get hurt. But in Bretzville, among my mother's German-American family, nothing violent ever, ever happened—a definite contrast to the fiery-tempered former Southerners who lived in Duff.

DUFFTOWN

Duff, or Dufftown, as it was originally named, actually began one mile south of its present location. A settlement of early pioneers, it was named after Colonel Bazil B. Edmonston, from Buncombe County, North Carolina. He was a founding father of the county, and was called Colonel Duff, presumably after Dufftown, Scotland. A Pimitive Baptist Church at Dufftown doubled as a subscription school and was surrounded by a cluster of cabins. When the railroad came in 1882, Robert C. Small, whose family also came from North Carolina, filed a plat for a couple of acres on his farm that lay next to the railroad, sold the lots, and Duff was underway.

As laid out, Duff consisted of only seventeen lots, bounded by First and Second Streets on the south and north, and Main and Nicholas Streets on the west and east. Nicholas Street was named after Nicholas Small, Robert's father. Nicholas and his wife Margry and their children left North Carolina in a covered wagon in 1833, traveling through the Cumberland Gap, bound for Indiana. On the night of November 13th, a tremendous number of stars fell (one of those times, every thirty-three years, when the Leonid meteor shower is particularly heavy) and the Smalls, a religious and superstitious people, became frightened and believed the falling stars were a heavenly sign that they should not go. After talking it over, they decided to wait another night, praying that if they were to turn back, they would be shown the stars one more night. No stars fell and they continued their trek to Indiana. (Their son Robert, the founder of Duff, was an infant on that trip.) The seventeen lots sold very quickly and soon frontage of land bordering the plat sold too, thus doubling the size of platted Duff.

During my era, Wayne Hall's store was located on the northwest corner of Second and Main. His and wife Tillie's residence connected to the store and lay south toward the alley. The alley ran east-west the length of the platted area, and most folks had their outhouses on the alley. Some even kept a few hogs in their back yards. Continuing south along Main Street to the corner and next to the railroad track, was Wayne Hall's tin garage. The garage blocked the vision of motorists approaching on both Main and First Streets, creating a blind corner. I was standing on the depot platform one day waiting for the noon train, when I saw Stanley Peach approach the corner in his Graham-Paige while Wayne Hall was traveling the opposite way in his Dodge truck. Both took the inside curve and collided head-on. They got out of their cars and Wayne said, "Doggone, Stan, I had the inside lane," and Stan, with his odd little laugh that sounded like "Kahune," said, "I guess we both did, Wayne." Due to their slow speed and the strength of the bumpers on those old vehicles, they had merely bounced back.

Continuing east along First Street, one approached Charlie Spurlock's store and residence. Turning north on Nicholas Street, at its intersection with Second Street, was the residence of L.C. Brown, a telegrapher on the railroad. He was eccentric and curious, and in his upstairs room were many gadgets that I found interesting to see and touch. There was a telescope, a microscope, and a small, hand-powered generator, the kind used to power the telephone system. L.C. was an agnostic, while his wife Bertha was a very religious woman with high morals. Their son, Gene, who was and is an important mentor in my life, is an interesting combination of the two of them. Now retired in Minnesota, his love of Duff and its people also calls him home from time to time. Then turning the corner at the Brown residence and continuing west along Second Street, you arrived back at Wayne Hall's store—a quick tour of Duff.

We had no town government, and the only official we were ever to see was the county sheriff, who came only when some terrible mishap, intentional or accidental, had occurred. He showed up two or three times during those years. The townspeople rallied together and did what they needed to do following a natural disaster,

Birdseye view of Duff: 1) Duff School, 2) Songer Homeplace, 3) Ed Ermert's blacksmith shop, 4) Wayne Hall's store, 5) Baseball diamond, 6) Depot and Southern Railway, 7) Charles Spurlock store and Odd Fellows Hall, 8) Hugo Lemond's farm.

catastrophe, or an epidemic. Some folks had leadership skills which came to the fore when necessary, and most had a strong instinct to help their fellow human beings. It was a tightly knit bunch of people when death came unexpectedly, a house or barn burned, or a child was deathly sick.

We were isolated. The roads were bad in winter and automobiles were scarce. Getting a ride was always a daunting task. So, the people walked. Housewives trod the dusty roads to Duff, carrying little coin purses containing their nickels, dimes, and quarters and grocery baskets hanging in the crook of their arms. They stopped to talk across the fence with Mom, who was always home working and not part of the town "news network" so that she could get caught up on the town gossip. Sometimes, as they walked along those dusty summer roads, they accepted rides on farm wagons. The jolt wagons were uncomfortable—the only desirable place to sit was beside the farmer on the springboard seat. But in summer, most of the farmers had hay frames on their wagon running gear and long wide boards which ran along each side of the hay frame made a comfortable ride. You would see her pass by—legs dangling, and a considerable length of brown stocking showing, very pleased about her good fortune in obtaining a ride.

Saturday was a big day for activities. Both storekeepers made a trip to Huntingburg for merchandise and you could hitch a ride with them, do your business and meet them at an agreed meeting place for the return home. If you missed them, you could scurry to the meat packing houses, where they made their last stop. Saturday night movies were a huge treat. I was a big fan of Gene Autry and his horse Champion and so were Bill and Alice Sunderman. If I could find a dime, I was off to see a double feature with them on Saturday night.

Conversations on the store porch often involved work and how to get there. After high school, I got a factory job in Huntingburg. Bud Fenneman had purchased a new Dodge truck, even though he had never learned to drive. Albert "Neighbor" Lohman, a fellow railroad section worker of Bud's, was his driver and Bill Mayo, another railroad worker, sat in the middle in the cab. I rode in the back of the pickup, a cold ride in winter. The factory where I worked was forever trying to get rid of its waste wood, and it made excellent kindling. I offered to load up the pickup for my fellow commuters, and they readily accepted. After work, I picked them up at the depot, and Bud liked my driving well enough that he promoted me to regular driver. Poor old Neighbor lost his driving job and took my place in the back of the pickup. For a time I rode to work in a Model A Ford with George Reinbold, a retired farmer who had taken a factory job. George was still a farmer at heart and all summer long, as we drove home, he commented on the crops growing in fields along the road. He went so slow and looked at the fields with such intensity that sometimes the motor would stall out or he would drive in the ditch.

Loafing at the stores was exclusively a male pastime—the women came in, got their groceries and left. Duff women didn't do much loafing—raising their families was a full-time, labor-intensive job. Except for visits over backyard fences, they made their visiting times productive with sewing circles and quilting parties. Sometimes the men went along. Everyone socialized at shivarees; dances; at school events—spelling contests, box socials, Christmas and last day of school programs and shows in the Odd Fellows Hall. Everyone was included, the drunks and the teetotalers, the reprobates and the church-goers, except possibly August Feller, the miser, who neither asked for nor gave anything.

LIFE AT HOME

Dad and Mom experienced a tragedy early in their marriage when their first born, Betty Jean, died at age three. By all accounts, she was a precocious child, given to adult mannerisms and speech. When she became ill, she didn't linger long. The doctor was mystified by her illness and within a week, she was gone. Dad said many times that it took him seven years to get over her death. I'm not sure what he meant. My guess is that he suffered internally and his behavior was affected by her death. The next oldest was Katherine Louise Clara; then myself; then another daughter, Mary Ann, named for her great grandmother; then James Louis, named after both grandfathers; then three more girls, Janice Sue, Judith May, and Carol Jane. We were all three years apart, except Carol who followed Judy by only two years. All of us could carry a tune, and our main recreation as a family was singing. Mom taught us songs from World War I and hits from the flapper era of the 1920s. At least a few hundred times we gathered on our front porch and sang late into the evening. People at Duff said, "We heard the Songers singing again last night." When brother Jim was twelve years old, Mom scraped together enough money to buy him a cheap, mail-order guitar. She taught him the three chords she knew, and soon Jim was on his way to becoming the musician in the family.

Our upstairs had two rooms; my sisters shared one, and Jim and I the other. We slept on mattresses filled with corn shucks, and covered ourselves with featherbeds. The upstairs was unheated and very cold in winter. It was also hot in summer. In 1936, the year of the great dust bowl in the West, when sweltering summer temperatures exceeded one hundred degrees on a daily basis, we moved our mattresses out to the front porch and slept there. Day after day, as the landscape sizzled and cracked under the boiling hot sun, we lay on blankets spread on the grass under the maple trees, where we tried to catch an occasional breeze. Overhead, parched, gray-green leaves of

Hugo E. and Clarissa (Bretz) Songer Family

Front: Mary Ann, James Louis, Janice Sue, Judith Mae, Carol Jane.
Rear: Hugo Charles, Hugo Elijah, Clarissa Amalia, Katherine Louise Clara, holding her daughter Rita Astrike.

the drought-stricken maples rattled like the dry leaves of Fall when a hot breeze came through.

On July 4th of that year, we were picnicking under those trees when an east-bound freight suddenly screeched to a stop. Dad and I hurried to a point just west of the Duff crossing where people had gathered, and there we saw the ghastly grisly remains of Leroy Lampert, who had been cut lengthwise into two parts, one part lying between the rails and the other on the outside. Someone felt this scene too grotesque and obscene an arrangement, so the two halves were placed together on the grass next to the track. Whether Leroy failed to hear the onrushing train, or decided to end his earthly existence on that Independence Day, no one knew, nor would ever know.

We had an outhouse, a two-holer of the home-made variety, which sat under cherry trees northeast of the house. Invariably, the trees yielded a most beautiful and bountiful crop of cherries each year and I never gave any thought concerning why that was. There was a chamber pot upstairs for our use, which one of us had to carry downstairs each morning. One morning, one of the girls who shall remain unnamed, slipped and spilled the pot at the top of the stairway and the defecates went rolling and thunking down the stairs, creating one more horrible mess for Mom to clean up! "Oh my God," Mom groaned, hands covering her face. She wasn't really angry, just in total despair. But she never would embarrass us when we accidentally did something like that. Swiftly and without another word, she just handled it.

Our farm consisted of eighty-four acres, twenty-four of which lay on the east side of the road, next to Duff, and the remaining sixty on the west side of the road, north of the school. The twenty-four acres lay okay, but the sixty across the road were hilly, except for a stretch of branch bottom, and far better suited for pasture than row crops. While Dad wasn't much of a farmer, he was a very hard worker. Grandpa wasn't much of a farmer either, but he always had an outside source of income which Dad didn't have, and besides, Dad had to contend with the mortgage on the farm placed there by Grandpa.

Dad became extremely frustrated, and his temper would boil over when things went wrong. When a cow or calf, or a hog or horse died, it was a major blow, especially when you operated as close to the margin as we did. The equipment was all horse-drawn and our horses were of medium quality. One early, muddy spring day, Dad was hauling manure which had accumulated in the barn over the winter. Under soggy conditions and with a load on, the steel wagon tires mired into the mud. The horses pulled hard, but had great difficulty moving the load. Dad stood on the front of the wagon and whipped them with the ends of the reins. Suddenly, one of the horses fell dead. His frustration is easy to understand. There was a pressing need to clean out the barn and scatter manure on the fields before spring plowing, there were dozens of other spring chores to do, and one of his horses was lying dead in its harness.

Cash was a scarce commodity, so Dad decided to raise a tomato crop for a local cannery. A couple of acres of tomatoes in the branch bottom should do the trick. He plowed the ground, dragged, disced, and harrowed it, and the entire family was involved in putting out the tomato plants. A few days later, a minor flood washed them out, and we replanted only to have them washed out again. Damn the luck! In spite of the setbacks, we managed to get in a few acres of corn, wheat, and oats every year. After harvest, we fed a considerable portion of the crop to our animals. The rest we hauled to town and sold for cash. I dearly loved those trips to Huntingburg, perched atop a wagon load of sacked wheat and oats. Dad was sitting on the springboard seat of the wagon, hunched over the reins, occasionally slapping the back of a lagging horse with the reins. It was a long, unhurried trip on a rarely traveled dirt road.

Farm work was a never ending activity for the entire family. One of my chores was feeding the animals in the barn. In winter, when it got dark early, I went to the barn with a lantern. Often the night sky was beautiful, stars shining in great clusters and looming so large it appeared I could reach up and pluck them from the sky. The barn was a wonderful place in winter. Its sights, sounds, and smells captivated me: cows' eyes gleaming in soft lantern light as they silently chewed their cuds; the sweet, mingled aroma of cow's breath, timothy hay, and horse manure; the horses stomping, registering their impatience to be fed; and the stirring of a few independent-minded roosters who had rejected life in the chicken house and found a home in the barn. Body heat from the animals raised the barn temperature several degrees warmer than the outside, and I found it easy to linger a while before returning to the house.

I witnessed the greatest sight of my life on a cloudless, sunny afternoon as I crossed the barnlot. A rumbling sound, the likes of which I had never heard, was coming from overhead in the northeast. We were unaccustomed to seeing anything flying in the sky except birds, bats, and Frosty Jones. I looked up just in time to see an object larger than the barn nosing into view. It was a dirigible, which I had seen only in pictures, flying low, right over our barn! It was the largest object I had ever seen and I was overwhelmed by its size and magnificence. I yelled and screamed, desperately wanting to share the view of a lifetime with someone else, but it disappeared over Duff before I could rouse anyone from the house. It was the topic of conversation on the store porch for several days, and those of us who had seen this most magnificent sight held center stage as we related what we had seen to those who hadn't.

Each spring, a couple of hundred baby chicks came in on the local and were placed in our brooder house. Inside, the floor was covered with bark, and a small coal stove kept the place toasty warm—about eighty degrees. The stove was equipped with a crude brass thermostat containing a vacuum that expanded and contracted with the amount of heat, thus closing or opening the damper and keeping the temperature at a fair constant. Even so, Dad got up in the wee hours to check on things and add coal to the stove. The brooder house roof caught on fire once, but we got it out soon enough to save it and the chickens. When this flock of half roosters and half hens outgrew the brooder house, we transferred them to the chicken house a hundred yards away.

We didn't need a hundred roosters—one for every five or so hens would do, so when the roosters, called springers, grew to two pounds or so, Mom would say every Sunday morning: "Go catch a couple of springers." We picked out the two largest ones we could find and literally ran them down. Under the locust trees, there was a chopping block with two nails driven in it. Mom placed the springer's head between the nails and chopped its head off with an axe. I was fascinated to watch them run five or six steps, headless, before flopping to the ground. They were thrust into a bucket of scalding hot water to make feather plucking easier.

As the hens matured and began laying eggs, one of our chores was to feed the chickens and gather and grade the eggs every evening. We gathered nearly a hundred a day, and at the end of the week, a hatchery would pick them up—our main source of cash money. Raising chickens wasn't automatic; we had to compete with predators who also liked our chickens and eggs. More than once, I went down a dark row of nesting boxes where hens laid their eggs and without looking, reached in and grabbed a handful of chicken snake which had crawled into the box to eat the eggs. Sometimes hawks swooped down and carried off a chick (all hawks were chicken hawks to us).

Another time, I walked into the chicken house and it looked like a murder scene. Eleven grown hens lay there, lifeless and pale as if the very blood had been sucked from them. I gathered several dead chickens in each hand and started for the house, yelling, "Dad, Dad, something's killing our chickens." He came running toward the chicken house while I hurried through the barnlot with my load of dead chickens. Then I heard him yell, "Charlie, bring your gun. Whatever's killing the hens is still in here." I grabbed my rifle and ran back to the chicken house, stepped in and Dad said, "Under the roost." I knelt down and saw a dark animal running left to right along the back wall. I led the streaking animal and fired, and it fell dead. It was a mink and it had in fact only wanted the hens' blood.

Sometimes the predators were human. Young, single men with no money, nothing to do, and nowhere to go, would decide to have a chicken fry on Saturday night. They stole chickens from local farmers and took them to a remote spot where they fried them over an open fire. Our chickens were raising a ruckus one night and the dog, Nipper, was going crazy too. Dad got up, loaded his shotgun, and went outside. Clearly, someone or something was in the chicken house so he fired into the air and yelled, "Get out of my chicken house or I'll come down there and shoot you in the ass." Two figures darted out and as Dad fired again, they left a gunny sack containing three chickens stranded on our barbed wire fence.

One should really describe life with electric power and life without. They were two entirely different ways of life. Until 1943, before power, we carried water into the house for all purposes a bucket at a time, used an outhouse, lit the house with kerosene lamps, and listened to a battery-powered radio crackle and pop. Mom did the washing on a washboard—outside under the locust trees in summer, and in the kitchen in winter. In inclement weather, the newly washed clothes hung from a clothes-line rope that zigzagged across the living room, creating a maze. Ironing was done with so-called sad irons, which were alternately heated on the stove, and used until they cooled, then exchanged for a hot one.

We heated the house with a wood stove in the living room, switching to a coal stove when life became more prosperous. In the evening, after supper, while Mom and my sisters washed the dishes (my job was to keep the water bucket full), Dad retired to the living room and listened to H.V. Kaltenborn or Lowell Thomas give their version of the news, then turned the radio dial to Amos and Andy or Fibber McGee and Molly; the faint yellow light of the radio dial the only light in the room. When Joe Louis fought, we all gathered around the radio. It seemed like every time things got really exciting, and Joe was about to dispatch another victim to never-never land, static erupted and we crowded closer to the radio, straining to hear and asking each other what happened.

After finishing my chores, I joined Dad in the living room and played under the bed with a toy truck with battery-powered headlights, wrestled with my little brother Jim, or crawled on Dad's lap where he "whiskered" me. When Mom and the girls finished cleaning the kitchen and washing dishes, only then did they bring the lamp into the living room. If we had home-work to do, we sat on the stair-steps, using a cabinet sewing machine for a table. Mom sat nearby, sewing patches on clothes and darning socks. Always, always, working. Mom was the hardest working person I have ever known. She not only washed all our clothing by hand on a washboard—she took in washing for the cash it brought in. She raised a large garden, canned hundreds of quarts of fruits and vegetables, milked cows, supervised us children in our tasks, cooked a hot meal three times a day, baked bread every few days (Dad wouldn't touch store-bought), cleaned our house and the houses of others for cash money, and still had time for opening exercises at school. I don't know how she got it all done without electric power.

In 1942 we got the news that rural electrification was on its way and that those who wanted electric power could get it. At first, Dad didn't want it, but when he learned what all it could do for us and that a large percentage of our neighbors were going to hook on, he changed his mind. He went to work for the electric utility digging postholes at twenty-five cents per hole, having been supplied with a great long posthole digger, the longest I had ever seen, to dig the holes six feet deep. He could dig an average of eleven a day, but sometimes could not achieve that average when he hit a layer of sandstone and was required to pound his way through it. Raymond Reinbold wired our house in 1943; we received word that at a certain hour on a given day, the power was to be turned on. When the time for the magical event arrived, I ran from room to room switching the lights on and off, marveling at the creation of instant light, especially when compared to cleaning the soot covered lamp globes, filling them with smelly kerosene, trimming wicks and lighting them with a match. Electric appliances were expensive so we started small. First came an electric iron and that was pretty exciting, but I will never

In front of Songer homeplace: from left–Adults, Norma Lohman, Laney Lutsgesell (Lena Lemond), Mae Osborn, Leona Mayo, Ollie Fisher, Clarissa Songer, Amelia Martin; children, Carol and Judy Songer.

forget the day when a new washing machine was delivered via the local. We were all happy but Mom was absolutely ecstatic!

After electric power came, Mom had more leisure time and while the washing machine was running, she would talk over the fence with Mae Osborn as she walked by. That's how Mom caught up on the news. Somehow or other, even though Mae lived a half mile north of Duff, she was up on all the gossip. "Oh Creesey," she would declaim, after relating some incident, "It's so awful!"

Mae was a very kind person, particularly to us kids, perhaps because she had not raised any of her own. She had given birth to a child however, a daughter, conceived as the result of Mae's having been raped when she was a young girl. Mae loved her little girl but Alas! the child died when she was three, drawing her last breath on a silk pillow. Mae cherished that pillow and kept it in the center of her bed. She allowed us to look at it as she told us about her daughter but we were never allowed to touch the sacred silk pillow.

Mae's husband Norm was the local carpenter. If you needed a house or shed built, Norm was your man. Once when I was nine or ten years old, I was visiting the Lemond boys, Ed, Pete and Jim, who lived next to Norm. Norm's geese were swimming on his pond, so we threw rocks into the pond to scare them. The rocks didn't seem to bother them, so I picked up a rock as large as my fist and gave it a mighty heave. We all watched it arch into the air and then descend squarely on the head of a large white goose. At first we thought it was funny, but as the goose thrashed around in the water, it soon became clear that the goose was mortally wounded. We scurried away from there, hoping Norm hadn't seen us. That afternoon, on his way to Duff, Norm stopped at our yard gate and told Mom that the boys had killed one of his geese. I told Norm that Pete Lemond did it, and he left, satisfied that was true. The next day he was back again, and informed Mom and me that the Lemond boys said that I was the deadly rock-thrower. I had to own up to it. Norm didn't say much and wouldn't accept payment for the goose. Then Mom and I had a talk. She took me to the barn where no one would interrupt us. I remember the exact spot I was standing. She didn't mention the goose but homed right in on the lie. She said she was ashamed of me and was tempted to call the sheriff right then and have me put in jail because I had committed one of the worst crimes there is—lying, and if it ever happened again, I would definitely go to jail. I was very ashamed and decided right then that lying was no way to get out of a bad spot.

In the morning, Mom was the first up. During summer, I too would hurry to the kitchen in the morning to stand at the east window and watch morning glorys Mom had planted open their dewy faces to the rising sun. In winter, the door to the kitchen was closed overnight and the kitchen range fire allowed to die. I was awakened by the sound of stovelids being thrown off the kitchen range as Mom prepared to build a fire with corn cobs, kerosene, and kindling. I got up, went down-stairs, and stuck my skinny butt against the rod which ran across the front of the stove. Often, there was a skim of ice on the water in the cedar water bucket. But within minutes, a hot breakfast of eggs, ham, gravy, and biscuits helped us start the day. A real whirling dervish of a worker, and a remarkable, wonderful woman, my mother!

Dad, like his forefathers, was a drinker. He didn't drink every day, but it's safe to say he drank every weekend, particularly after he went on "public works." On Friday, payday, he and fellow workmen would gather at the taverns in Huntingburg. He was a cinch to come home late. Mom's irritation showed only in the manner in which she rattled pots and pans as she began the evening meal. When I heard his car roll into the shed, I went out and more often than not, he had a bottle of muscatel. He always offered me a drink, took one last big swig himself, and then we went to the house. Sometimes his mood remained affable and sometimes it didn't—it was difficult to know which it would be. One night he came home really late—after midnight. I heard a commotion on the porch so I went downstairs and opened the door. He had one knee on the window sill and was running his hand up and down the glass, saying: "I always wanted a glass door and now it looks like I've finally got one, but where in the hell is the door knob?"

In summer, Mom prepared family meals on the kerosene stove on the screened-in porch and we ate at a large table out there. Three of us sat on a bench which we reached by crawling through the open window between the kitchen and the porch. The youngest child at the time sat on a high chair at the corner of the table between Mom and Dad. After Dad finished eating, he would turn his chair on one leg, lean back against the wall, pull a Bull Durham sack from his bib overalls and roll a cigarette. Then he started a narrative, a monologue, about the events of the day or about life in general. He'd say, "Ah, a poor man doesn't have a chance. Look at so-and-so, living up there on the hill in that big fifteen-thousand dollar house. He doesn't have a care in the world." That was always the figure Dad used when he described someone as rich. Or, having lost his independence when he left the farm, he'd say: "Ah this damned public works, somebody is always telling you what to do," and he would cite a few examples that happened that day at work. In some ways Dad could have been a better man. However, when one considers how he had been spoiled as a young man, never permitted to do any hard work and yet how hard he worked, particularly during the Depression to raise seven children and see them all achieve a high school education, I think he did quite well.

TREED

During the Depression, our subsistence farming was done with animals, particularly the horses, which were someone else's rejects. We had a blind, black mare named Nell; a pair of branded, roan westerns named Bill and Barney; and an old bay mare named Daisy who ran around with her tail in the air. That habit proved her undoing when young Harold Sunderman who was working for Dad at wheat-threshing time, pulled a wagon load of wheat bundles too close to the separator, and poor Daisy, tail in the air, got it caught in the main pulley. With every revolution of the pulley, Daisy's rear end was lifted off the ground. It almost tore off her tail, but Gilbert Sunderman, the threshing machine operator, slapped a hand full of axle grease on the wound and she soon recovered.

Much later, she became old and sick, and while my mother was leading her to the watering trough, Daisy collapsed and died. In her death throes, she kicked in the well curb and almost fell in the well. Old Nell, the blind horse, got too old to find sufficient feed to keep her going, so Dad called the tankage company to come after her. I should not have been watching from the school yard when the dead truck operator pulled into our barnlot, led Nell from her stall to a point behind his truck and proceeded to hit her in the head with an ax, after which he winched her lifeless body into the "dead truck." It hurt my heart to watch. But Dad bought another western, and we finally had a good team until Barney, the taller and stronger of the two, stepped on a rusty nail, caught lockjaw, and died.

The machinery was, if anything, worse. The plow, drag, and harrow were all right, because they had no moving parts. But the corn planter and wheat drill, and particularly the binder were always breaking down. As the name suggests, the binder was designed to cut the wheat or oats, tie it in bundles, and after a rack on the rear had accumulated six or eight bundles, toss them off into a pile. Another worker would come along and build the bundles into a shock. The difficulty was, our binder was temperamental, and did not always "bind," or tie. It simply accumulated enough wheat straws to make a bundle, and then tossed the pile onto the ground, requiring the wheat shocker to manually tie each bundle, which slowed the process considerably. Dad went into a tirade, shouting, "Binder, binder, that son-of-a-bitch is no binder. It's a God-damned wheat cutter. Where in the God-damned hell did they get the word binder for that son-of-a-bitch. I oughta just sell the God-damned thing for junk." Matter of fact he had it right—it was a piece of junk. He finally cooled off and tinkered around with it so that it started tying again. When the bowl wheel, a large cleated wheel which was in contact with the ground and drove the moving parts, ran into a wash on hilly ground and broke a drive chain, again he vented his rage. I knew from experience that it was best to stand back and nod in agreement until his tirade ran its course.

Desperate to raise more money, Dad decided to go into the hog business in a big way. He bought a boar and a couple of sows and began raising hogs. Like many of our enterprises, this one did not do well, although as far as I know, it was no fault of ours. When the first litter came along, the sow died and we were required to hand feed a dozen baby pigs. Then about the time they were ready for market, they bunched up in the hog house one warm spring night, overheated, caught pneumonia, and all but the runt, died. The boar, one sow, and the runt were all that was left of the hog business. Around the same time, we lost a horse, and a cow and calf. That just about finished Dad and farming. He wasn't much of a farmer anyway. The war drums in Europe were heating up, jobs were getting easier to find, and he announced he was going to quit farming and go to public works. To Dad, when he worked for someone else, he was doing "public works."

One summer day, Mom, Sis, and I had gone to the barn to do

some chores. As we left the barn and were about to return to the house, Mom yelled, "My God, the boar is out." This was no ordinary boar. He weighed about five hundred pounds and had a long tusk extending upward from each side of his mouth. He was mean. When I stood on the fence surrounding the pen, and he fastened his beady eyes on me, I was simultaneously repelled and fascinated at his brute power. Mom yelled for us to climb on top of a wheat fan which stood beside the barn, while she ran another direction, mother quail fashion, in order to distract the boar from us. The boar knocked Mom to the ground and gored her on the thigh. About that time the bread man, who was passing by and saw what was happening, grabbed a board lying by the fence and beat the boar off Mom, giving her time to scramble to her feet and get behind a nearby locust tree. While the boar had his attention fixed on Mom, the bread man yelled for Sis and me to make a dash for the yard gate, which we did, and we set a record for barn-to-yard-gate dashing. Meanwhile, Mom was able to gain the yard and now that we were all safe inside the yard fence, the bread man left, and we began discussing what to do next. After we caught our breath and determined that the cut on Mom's leg was not very serious, Mom told me to go tell Uncle Tom what happened, and ask him to come and get the boar back in his pen, because Dad would not get home from work until later that afternoon.

Uncle Tom Songer was my Grandpa's brother, and my favorite great-uncle. The youngest child of Floyd and Mary Ann, he was only fourteen when they divorced. When he was seventeen, he was charged with and convicted of carrying a concealed weapon, and at age twenty-one, charged with attacking a locomotive. Apparently, Uncle Tom had fired a couple of shots at a passing locomotive, for the reason that his girlfriend, Lena Lemond had boarded the engine and was taking a short ride on the local to entertain the engine crew, and Uncle Tom didn't like it. His brother Jim, (Grandpa) signed his bond, hired an attorney to represent him, and after a trial, he was acquitted because the engineer and fireman could not be found in the bailiwick to testify. When he was twenty-seven, after he and Iva Aust were convicted of the crime of fornication and fined ten dollars each, they married and moved away from Duff and he was gone for many years.

He served some time in an Illinois jail for making moonshine whiskey and for a while, went under the alias of Tom Fisher. He once told me that for seven years, he didn't draw a sober breath. "The first thing I did when I swung my legs out of bed in the morning was to reach under the bed where I kept a jug and take a big swig. Then I was ready to start the day." When he returned to Duff in early 1939, he had quit drinking, but Mom didn't know that and when we looked toward the barn where Dad was doing the chores and saw Uncle Tom following Dad from stall to stall, Mom became visibly upset, saying that Dad didn't need another drinking buddy. He began looking for a place to live, and when he learned that Laney Lotsgesell (Lena Lemond) was widowed, (her husband Adam had been gassed in World War I and only now died of it) Uncle Tom sought her out, ready to take up where he had left off many years before. The difficulty was that a man named Basham was living with Laney. Uncle Tom was not to be deterred this time and told Basham, "Hitch up your mules to your wagon, load up your stuff and move out because I'm moving in." Uncle Tom always wore the same old sweat-stained Stetson, bib overalls, pant legs rolled halfway to his knees, and work socks and shoes. All the Songers had big noses, and Uncle Tom the biggest. He wore "long handled" underwear year round, with the sleeves of his blue denim shirt rolled up to his elbows over his long underwear. When I arrived there, Uncle Tom and a hired hand, Spatsy Barnett, nicknamed after the diminutive bird, were hoeing a watermelon patch. (Uncle Tom bragged when he returned to Duff that he was going to raise watermelons that would be too big for me to straddle). After I told them what happened, Uncle Tom said, "Come on Spatsy, let's go take care of that old boar." We jumped in Uncle Tom's Model T truck and flivvered off down Laney's lane, which came out on the main rock road just north of the school yard near our house.

They armed themselves with boards and approached the boar in an attempt to herd him back toward his pen. But the boar, apparently relishing new-found freedom, charged, and Uncle Tom and Spatsy found themselves on the defensive before they could even swing their boards. The boar was between them and the yard gate so they had to run in the opposite direction. Uncle Tom yelled, "Look out Spatsy, and run like hell for them pear trees." They ran toward the pear trees near the chicken house, Uncle Tom climbing one and Spatsy the other.

There they sat, all afternoon, like two old treed coons, with the boar grunting and circling menacingly below. We shouted words of encouragement from the yard fence, like "Hold tight," and "Don't fall out," but could think of no way to help them out of their situation except to wait for Dad to get home. By the time he arrived, the old boar's hunger apparently overcame his desire to remain near his quarry in the pear trees, and after some herding by Dad with one of the discarded boards, the boar returned to his pen. Deciding the boar was too dangerous to keep, Dad took him to Hill Top Packing Company the very next day, where he was made into sausage. Fortunately, Uncle Tom and Spatsy were not injured, except for their pride, but their reputation as livestock handlers was considerably damaged. They preferred not talking about it on the store porch in Duff.

BUTCHERING HOGS

In late November or early December, as the weather turned sharp, Dad began preparing for another significant annual event—butchering hogs. He built a platform of rough lumber, with holes for two barrels which were set at an angle. We gathered enough wood to feed the fires for a day, laid the fires, built a couple of tripods across which was placed a horizontal bar about six feet from the ground, and arranged for a crew to help with the work. Otto Weisheit, a neighboring German farmer, was the main butcher, Uncle Tom would be there, and my maternal grandmother, Katherine Bretz, helped Mom. I was the go-fer.

We arose about 4:00 am and started the fires under the kettles so that the water would be boiling by daylight. The sausage grinder and lard press had been cleaned and were standing by, butcher knives were sharpened and laid out, and several five gallon lard cans were set out to the side. As the first streaks of light spread across the barn lot, the crew assembled. Three hogs had been isolated in a nearby pen, and we were ready to begin. The first task was to shoot the hogs. That was Uncle Tom's job. He said, "Charlie, I'll shoot the first one and you can shoot the other two. You want to shoot them squarely between the eyes about an inch above the line between them. That way, they will drop without a squeal." He continued, "I have shot hundreds of hogs, and never in my life have I made one squeal." I was a little apprehensive when faced with such a perfect record, but said, "OK," so Uncle Tom took careful aim at the first hog and at the very instant he pulled the trigger, the hog turned its head, and Uncle Tom shot it through the left ear. Well, the hog ran around the small pen, squealing its head off, with a small black hole it its ear, while Uncle Tom stood there in open-mouthed amazement at this turn of events. However, he quickly regained his composure and skillfully dispatched all three hogs.

As each hog was shot, it was stuck in the throat with a knife to drain the blood, dragged to the platform, and with a strong man on each hind leg, shoved into the barrel which was by now filled with hot water, and moved back and forth. This process sterilized the skin and made it easier to remove the hair. After the hair was scraped off, the hog was hung on the horizontal bar, gutted, and the body propped open so that the carcass could cool. At this point, we took a break.

It was said that when the German farmers butchered, they saved everything but the squeal. That included the blood, which was made into blood sausage, or "blut wurst." But Dad didn't like it, so we made no attempt to save the blood. We did, however, save the stomach and the intestines, large and small, when Otto gutted the hogs. Mom and her helpers turned the intestines inside out with a stick, scraped them with a piece of wood, and soaked them in salt water, thus getting them ready to fill with sausage. The stomach was filled with "head cheese," which was meat scraped from the skull and included the ground up heart and kidneys.

After the carcasses cooled, Otto began carving them into hams, shoulders, sides, and jowls; the tenderloins were cut away; the fat stripped and cut into squares for rendering into lard, and lean meat not part of the hams and shoulders was dropped into the sausage grinder to be made into sausage. After it was ground, the women began making sausage. Otto, who had a widely known reputation for sausage making, applied the seasoning. The sausage was placed into the press and the casings (cleaned intestines) were placed on a spout so that when the sausage came out the spout under pressure, it filled the casings into a continuous stream of sausage. Meanwhile, the squares of fat, filling two tubs, were dumped into the now empty kettles, the fire built back up, and lard rendering began. The boiling fat was stirred with a wooden ladle until much of the lard had been boiled out; then the squares were ladled into the lard press to squeeze out the remaining lard. This left cracklins, which were a delicious snack after they cooled. When the lard was poured into lard cans, it was amber colored; after it cooled, it became a beautiful color of pure white. Recalling the butchering process reminds me of a song we used to sing on the front porch:

There was a great big German man
Whose name was Donner Beck
And he was fond of poodle dogs
And sauer kraut and speck (sausage)
He had a great big butcher shop
The finest ever seen
He got himself a patent
To make sausage by machine
One night the machine was broken
And wouldn't work it out
So Donner Beck, he crumpled in
To find the matter out
His wife was having nightmares
And walking in her sleep
She gave the crank one hell of a yank
And Donner Beck was meat.

That evening, all the helpers stayed for supper which the women had been preparing all day. Traditionally, we had fresh tenderloin and sausage, along with mashed potatoes, sauerkraut and gravy, green beans, hot home-made rolls, and canned blackberries–a real feast. The next day, the hams, shoulders, and sides were salted and in a few days, the smoking process began. A tub was filled half full of ashes to keep it from burning through, a fire was started in the tub, and after it got going, green hickory wood was placed on the fire, and the tub was carried into a room of the house called the back kitchen where the meat was hanging. For a week, the smoldering fire, which emitted lots of hickory wood smoke, was kept going. After the smoking process was complete, the hams were hung from a pole suspended from the ceiling of the back kitchen. That completed the process of butchering, and all winter long, as cold winds whipped around the house, we ate our supply of meat. The hams were the most delicious, of course, but we were required to eat a shoulder in its turn, and it was a cause for celebration when Mom announced it was time to cut into another ham.

ED ERMERT

Ed Ermert's blacksmith shop was halfway to Duff, roughly a city block south of our house. One of the most important men in the community, Ed shod horses and mules, sharpened plowpoints, repaired farm wagons, put new tires on wagon wheels, and repaired clay mine cars and Model T and Model A cars. He was argumentative and opinionated, but I liked him and he liked me. When I walked into his shop, he would say *Wie gehts allaweil* or

Charlie, Charlie, I've been thinking
What a queer world this would be
If all the Charlies were transferred
Across the wide and deep blue sea

Ed was short and powerfully built, with a round face and thinning hair. Suspenders held up his pants and he rolled his shirtsleeves to his elbows. When something struck him funny, he would rear back his head and laugh uproariously. He also roared with anger and indignation just as easily when things didn't suit him. Ed's family immigrated from Germany when he was four years old. He took up the blacksmithing trade as a young man, married and had four children. In 1916, his wife Sophie died and Ed, with four small children to care for, needed a wife. So he married Sophie's sister Carrie and had three more children. His son Chalk was a year older than me, and we spent some time together growing up.

Ed's shop, made of tin, was shaded from the hot afternoon sun by the canopy of a huge oak across the road. Outside, all along the front of the shop, was a tangle of iron of all shapes and sizes which Ed used to fashion needed parts. He always knew exactly where he could locate the desired piece of iron. Inside, there was a forge, which was

Ed Ermert, blacksmith; Hugo Lemond, farmer.

on the end of the shop nearest the road, and on the other end of the shop was a "donkey" engine which provided the power for his drill press, grinder, and band saw. I was fascinated by many things in his shop, but the item that intrigued me most was the hoist consisting of two steel pulleys, one slightly larger than the other, and a chain. One pulley was tied into the rafters, so that when a car was brought into the shop for repair, and needed to be hoisted, Ed merely hooked the other pulley on the bumper, and by pulling on the loose chain from the top pulley, lifted one end of the car in the air. He often allowed me to do it, and I was intrigued by the fact that with the leverage provided by the pulleys and chain, I could lift the front end of a car.

When Ed was dealing with a stubborn mule or a newly tempered piece of iron that wouldn't fit, he could get very frustrated by his work. However, nothing got to him quite like putting new tires on wagon wheels. The iron tires had to be heated so that they would expand enough to be hammered onto the wooden rim of the wheel. The tires were heated red hot in a circular fire which was built outside the shop, and usually tended by Carrie. Son Elmer had long since learned better than to get involved and made himself scarce on wagon wheel tire days. The tire was removed with tongs, and hammered onto the wheel. If it didn't slide on immediately, Ed was in trouble, because the tire soon began to cool and contract. The air became blue with Ed's swearing, usually directed at Carrie for not keeping the fire hot enough. I learned to stay way back out of the way on such days.

Carrie possessed mystical powers. She could stop bleeding, take the fire out of burns, and treat minor wounds by the generous application of "coal oiler" (kerosene). She wore her salt and pepper hair in a shoulder length bob and had a constant tremor which caused her head to move continuously from side to side. On a hot June day, when I was seven, we were putting up hay and my job was to keep the workers supplied with fresh, cold water. I had crossed the road to the school house well, where the water was fresher and colder, to fill a glass gallon jug when I accidentally dropped the jug on the concrete well curb and it shattered into pieces. I picked up the larger pieces, and held them in my cupped hands next to my chest. On my way across our yard, I stumbled over a croquet wicket and a spear shaped piece of glass pierced my throat. I began bleeding heavily. It was clear to everyone that I needed a doctor. At that time we had a car, but it wouldn't start, so someone went after Ed Ermert's car. It wouldn't start either because it was out of gas. I asked Mom several times if I was going to die and each time, she assured me that I would not, but I could see the fear in her eyes. Meantime, Carrie had learned of my situation and stopped the bleeding. Finally, we arrived at the doctor's office and he sewed up the wound, expressing amazement at the minimal blood loss.

Another time, when my sister Kate removed a pot of boiling butter beans from the stove, she tipped the pot and scalded her hands. She was experiencing excruciating pain. Carrie was notified and came to our house, passed her hands over my sister's burns and relieved the pain immediately. No one knew whether Carrie called upon a higher power or recited an incantation when she exercised her power. Strange thing though; Carrie's son Elmer, had chronic strep throat. The treatment of choice then was to paint his throat with iodine but it made Carrie too squeamish so when Elmer had a throat infection, she sent him to Mom to have his throat painted.

As she grew old, she informed her children that she could pass the power on to a male child only. She had three sons—the eldest, Henry, lived in St. Louis and was not available; Elmer lived in the area, but for reasons of her own, Carrie did not want him to have the power. That left son, Chalk (Harold), but he refused to accept it. Apparently, Carrie was not happy with his decision. Both Chalkie and his wife, Mary Ella, said that on the night she died, someone knocked at their door. No one was there. The knocking continued and several times they answered the door but no one was there. They decided to stand right by the door in order to catch the someone or something who was knocking. When they jerked open the door, no one was there. Then the knocking began to occur within interior walls of the house and continued throughout the night and until Carrie was buried.

When Mom saw Carrie coming up the road to pay her a visit, she paid homage to Carrie's strangeness by saying, "Here comes the Old Owl." I never believed nor disbelieved—don't to this day. It was just part of life in Duff.

Wayne Hall, the storekeeper, and Ed once had a serious dispute. Afterwards, Wayne built his tin garage near the railroad track to spite Ed in an effort to take away his Model T repair business. But Ed was always on duty in his shop, while Wayne had to hire someone to repair cars, so Ed prevailed. For many years the old tin garage sat there on the corner next to the railroad track. There were a half dozen cars parked in there; some ran and some didn't. We young boys paused as we walked by and listened for the squeaking of springs, which were sometimes heard. It was mighty dark in there

No love was lost between Ed and Wayne. Once, after a particularly trying day putting on wagon tires, Ed was in Wayne's store and said he wanted to purchase some rope. Wayne grinned and asked, "Ed what do you plan to do with the rope?" and Ed, who probably thought it was none of his damned business, replied: "I'm so damned mad at Carrie for not keeping the fire hot, I am just going to take the rope to the barn loft, throw it over a beam and hang myself." Wayne grinned and said "Doggone, Ed, in that case, I'll just give you the rope."

Like Dad, Ed drank quite a bit. Dad was a strong Democrat and Ed an equally avid Republican. Ed didn't think much of the political process and politicians, and particularly Franklin D. Roosevelt. On election day, he walked to the polling place at Duff School just to write "Bullshit" across the paper ballot.

Ed and Dad went together to a community celebration in Ferdinand one day where Dad, carried away by whiskey and the patriotic fervor of the event, gave a passionate political stump speech. Ed, who had driven them to the event, got mad and went home without Dad. It took Dad quite awhile to find someone to bring him home, and when he arrived, he was blazing mad at Ed for leaving him stranded. He confronted Ed in front of his shop, and grabbed a piece of iron with which to whack him. In self defense, Ed picked up a hammer. They brandished their weapons and circled each other menacingly in Ed's driveway for a few minutes, shouting threats, but nothing more came of it except that they didn't speak to each other for four years!

It was awkward for us kids—we would drive by Ed's shop in the wagon and wave at Ed and he would wave back, but Dad stared straight ahead. Finally, Mom decided four years was long enough for the feud, so when she and Carrie decided to make pear butter, Mom providing the pears and Carrie the kettle, she insisted that Dad go along with her. Mom knew Dad and Ed were tired of the situation by this time and needed some way to end it. They didn't talk at first, but Mom said: "All right you two—four years is long enough—it's time you made up. There will be no discussion of politics or religion." She insisted they shake hands, and the air thus cleared, they resumed their neighborly relationship.

In 1950, Ed's youngest son, Chalk, bought a new Dodge. It was a beautiful car—dark green with white sidewalls, mudflaps, a sunvisor, and all the latest equipment. Ed decided to go to Colorado Springs to visit his daughter Selma and her family. Selma's husband Gilmore was a career soldier stationed at Camp Carson. I had been working a couple of years, had saved some money, and Ed and Chalk invited me to go along. I accepted immediately, already thinking about the sights I would see, especially the mountains. Furthermore, Chalk wanted me to help with the driving, because Ed didn't want to waste money on motels and we were going to drive straight through. Wow, a brand new Dodge!

We drove the major pioneer road, Highway 50. There were all sorts of attractions along the road, signs exhorting us to stop five miles down the road and see a strange animal which had been captured in some exotic foreign place, and as we got further west, to see a rattle-snake den, or a teepee with "genuine" Indians. Burma Shave signs entertained us on the long stretches through Kansas, where the endless wheat fields stretched away to the horizon. Each line of the limerick was painted on a wooden sign and the signs were about a hundred yards apart.

Cattle Crossing
Please Drive Slow
That old bull is
Some cow's beau

And

Her Chariot raced
At eighty per
They hauled away
What had Ben Hur
—Burma Shave

When we reached Colorado, I knew the mountains could not be far away, and even though I had driven through much of Kansas and was in need of sleep, I was determined to remain awake for that first glimpse of "the purple mountain majesty" that we had celebrated in song during opening exercises every morning at Duff school. At last, they came into view, and I was thrilled to see them stretching across the horizon, and was amazed at how many miles we had to travel before we were actually in them—the Rocky Mountains, the second greatest sight of my life. We saw the Garden of the Gods, the Will Rogers Shrine-of-the-Sun, the bridge across the Royal Gorge, said to be the highest suspension bridge in the world, and we toured the state prison at Canon City. We were led down long corridors of cells, each containing one prisoner, whose crime was set forth on a white card attached to the cell door. I was struck by how similar this was to a trip to the zoo, and was embarrassed to look into the eyes of the prisoners. Ed soon tired of touring and became homesick for Duff, so our trip was cut short after only one week of travel. On the return trip, while Ed and Chalk slept, I drove the entire length of Kansas, 520 miles! Later, we pulled into a park, and rolled the windows down in order to catch a breeze and an hour or so of sleep. Soon, we were slapping at mosquitoes and it was too hot with the windows up, so Ed declared, "Time to go back to Duff, boys," and away we went.

BLACKIE

We kept a few cows to provide our family with milk, cream, butter and cheese. On a small farm, with lots of children around, every animal had a name. There was "Lady" and "Betty," part Holstein; and "Jerse," the Jersey. Along with Dad, my sister Kate and I had spent a day walking barefoot down a dirt road to Pikeville, to buy that cow. The first mile was in the open, and bluebirds flitted from post to post among the honeysuckle and trumpet vines. Then we entered the woods, where squirrels and jays in the canopy overhead chattered their complaint at our passage, and the sand was cool under our feet. When we arrived at the home of Mrs. Corn, we found her in tears. As Dad handed her sixteen dollars and took the lead rope from her, she sobbed, "She's a good old cow and will give you all the milk you need. I wouldn't sell her but I'm getting too old to milk her." Dad promised to take good care of her and we led her home.

With the addition of Jerse, we had a herd of five cows. We usually pastured them in a hill field across the road and north of the rest of our farm. One of my chores was to find the cows every evening and drive them to the barn for milking. Customarily, I found them in a creek bed that ran through the woods at the far end of the forty-acre field. Sometimes my sister Mary Ann went with me and we paused to swing across the creek a few times on a grape vine we had cut.

The leader of the herd was "Blackie"—sort of the cur dog of cows. She had a pair of horns curving out of her head, pointing straight forward, like swords. Mary Ann was butted squarely in the stomach with those horns one day, but she wasn't seriously hurt. Blackie kicked the bucket over when she was being milked, and we sometimes questioned: why do we put up with that cow? Her milk was high in butterfat, and the cream, which we separated from the milk with a hand cranked separator, sold at a premium. Blackie's worst fault was that she didn't like to be led. This was a problem because we did not own a bull, and a cow must be bred every year to keep her fresh, that is, giving milk.

One evening after supper, after Dad turned his chair around on one leg, he leaned back against the wall, began rolling his Bull Durham cigarette, and sighed: "It's time to get Blackie bred. I've talked to Wayne Hall about it, and we are going to take Blackie to his bull. I've asked Ed Ermert to help." Dad didn't have to explain what all of us knew; Blackie was almost impossible to lead and Wayne kept his bull at his farm south of Duff across the railroad track! The next morning, Ed and his son Elmer showed up in Ed's Dodge truck, and we all went to Blackie's stall. It wasn't difficult to get a rope around her horns, but she resisted immediately. As soon as they let her out of the stall, it was clear that she was leading them—not the other way around. She ran into a pasture and started a mad gallop across the field with Dad taking long strides and Ed many little short ones in order to maintain a hold on the rope. Suddenly, she changed directions, "cracked the whip," and they sprawled end over end. They were both swearing and raising hell, Ed in particular, because this was his first experience with Blackie. As Blackie ran around the pasture trailing her rope, Ed ordered his son Elmer to "go get the old Dodge truck." Elmer got the truck, and after much effort Blackie was cornered and tied onto the rear.

Out of the barnlot and down the road to Duff we went, past a jeering crowd of loafers on Wayne Hall's store porch who were yelling things like: "can't you see that cow doesn't want to see the bull," and "how many farmers, blacksmiths, and boys does it take to lead a cow to the bull?" Dad, who realized what kind of picture we created, was embarrassed and yelled back, "Aw, go to hell." We continued across the railroad track, turning left into Wayne's pasture. We turned Blackie loose. The bull quickly became excited at this female newcomer and "covered" her three times, and then we were ready to return home. Meantime, Elmer, believing Blackie had learned her lesson and would not object to being led home, had returned the

Dodge home and walked back to Wayne's pasture. His theory proved correct until we reached the railroad track. Blackie refused to cross it. We tried to manhandle her over it and Dad and Ed were knocked down. Elmer, strong like an ox, even got behind her and tried to push to no avail. Finally, in a flash of inspiration, he yelled, "I'll make her go—I'll twist her tail." So he stood there, twisting her tail round and round, and Blackie stood there, hooves braced and bleeding, bellowing her protest at this assault on her dignity. Something had to give and something did. Suddenly there was a loud crack, and Elmer was standing there holding Blackie's tail, which he had twisted off. Elmer was very surprised, with an "Oh my God, what have I done" look on his face. He didn't know quite what to do, and made a halfhearted attempt to reattach it. At that point, Blackie bellowed again, took one great leap, cleared the railroad track, and headed for the barn. Long ago, I decided one couldn't have more fun than that on a summer afternoon.

WORK

Work was a family enterprise. We split kindling to start fires in the morning and sawed and chopped wood for the iron kitchen range and heating stove in the living room. A giant red oak on the east edge of our property went down during a storm, and Dad and I sawed and split it into stove-length pieces. We used a cross-cut saw eight feet long with a handle on each end. I had never used a cross cut saw before and like most tools, there is a knack to it. Dad always said, "don't push the saw back to me, son, and don't ride the saw. Just let it ride of its own weight and let the saw do the cutting. I'll do the same thing when you pull it back to your side." When he saw me using the ax or splitting maul and striking the piece of wood way off the mark, he explained: "You are a baseball player and a good hitter. Do you think you could hit that baseball if you were looking at some pretty girl on the sidelines? It's the same thing when you swing that ax. You have to concentrate on the exact place you want to strike the wood. In other words, you have to keep your eye on the ball!" I did much better after that. The ancient oak tree provided the entire wood supply for both stoves that winter.

The family garden was huge—potatoes alone covered a half-acre. Dad prepared the ground by plowing, discing, and harrowing. Then he "laid it off" into rows thirty inches apart. My job was to place the chunks of seed potatoes in the rows eight inches apart. "Make sure every piece of potato has an eye or there'll be no plant there." One of my sisters scattered fertilizer in the rows, and then we all grabbed hoes and covered the potatoes. After the potato plants came up, we used the hoes to pull dirt up to the plants on each side and create a hill of loose dirt where the young potatoes could thrive.

In September, Dad plowed the potatoes out with a one horse drawn plow. We picked them up, sacked them, and carried them to the empty brooder house or granary to dry. Since we had no cellar, before winter, we buried them to keep them from freezing. We dug a circular trench, and dirt from the trench was placed inside the circle, which had the intended effect of raising the dirt floor above ground level. A foot or so of straw was placed on that and then the potatoes were placed on the straw. Another foot of straw was added on top the potatoes, and then more dirt covered the whole thing. It began to take on the look of a cone. Old roofing tin kept the "cone" dry. Throughout the winter, we dug into the side of the cone to retrieve enough potatoes for a few weeks' supply, always carefully closing the hole so the potatoes didn't freeze. Ideally, we rooted around in there for the last few potatoes on the last day of freezing temperature.

We raised at least three hogs for butchering, and several cows for milk, which we consumed and sold. Of course, we had a few horses to provide power. All those animals had to be fed and cared for. The work was divided up although we children mostly took care of the animals; gardening and raising potatoes was a family effort. Fortunately for me (I always thought), my mother and sisters did the milking. I ran the separator, which separated cream from the milk. The separator was a hand-operated device with a crank, which was geared to spin a number of discs at high speed with the result that the heavier cream gravitated to the bottom and separated from the lighter skim milk. When the machine achieved the correct speed, whole milk was poured into a stainless steel bowl at the top. Soon, a stream of skim milk came out of one spout and golden cream came out the other. When the job was finished, the machine was taken apart and washed in hot water. It was important to reassemble the machine properly, and especially critical that the nut, which held the whole thing together, was tightly fastened. On one occasion, I failed to do so, and just as the discs achieved top speed, the moving parts of the machine came apart with a roar, discs flying in every direction, some leaving dents in the wall. I also delivered the still warm whole milk to a few customers in Duff.

Much of our food came from the garden. Mom canned green

beans, corn, beets, and peaches. In addition, she canned about one hundred quarts of blackberries, which grew wild on worn out land northwest of our farm. We had several favorite blackberry patches, all within a mile of our house. Getting up with the sun, we donned a couple of shirts and trousers to protect us from the briers, and headed for a patch we had not picked for a few days. Even though we didn't own the land, we had a proprietary attitude toward the blackberry patches and were irritated on rare occasions when some other picker had preceded us there. By midmorning, just as the sun had finished drying off the dew, we were ready to head for home with eight to ten gallons of blackberries. Some were canned, some made into preserves and jelly, and some sold for cash money. We took a warm, soapy bath in a washtub of water that had been left in the yard to be heated by the sun, thus being early users of solar heat. If we failed to do that, chiggers that had crawled aboard in the berry fields would chew on us for a week. The application of kerosene to our bodies helped too.

At age thirteen, I began working for area farmers. Rising early on Monday morning, I rode my bicycle to their farms, boarded with them during the week, and returned home on Saturday evening. My first employer was Jake Whitsitt, whose son Gilbert later married my sister Mary Ann. I'll never forget my first day. We harnessed three teams of horses that Monday morning, the team driven by Jake pulling a farm wagon on which we had loaded three moldboard plows, and headed for the Reddinbaugh bottoms located near the Postlethwaite covered bridge that spanned the Patoka River. A few years earlier, a portion of the bottoms had been cleared of its virgin timber, the logs sold and the tops piled and burned, leaving the stumps. We hitched our horses to the plows and began plowing the bottom ground. It wasn't long before we began hitting the stumps which were concealed just below the surface and there were a few moments of chaos when the plowpoint dug into one. The horses resented the shock of a sudden stop, and sometimes broke some portion of their harness. The plowman was bent over the plow handles by the impact, and the plowpoint became embedded in the stump. The only way to remove it was to move the plowhandles from side to side until the plowpoint came loose, then bear down on the plow handles, go up and over the stump until you struck another one.

At the end of an exhausting day, I was so tired I fell asleep in the wagon on the way to the Whitsitt homestead. Immediately after supper, I went to bed and awoke to the blissful sound of rain falling on the tin roof just over my head. I rolled over and slept some more, grateful in the knowledge that I would not be plowing new ground that day. At breakfast, Jake, who had retained the speech idioms of his eastern mountain Scottish ancestors, said, "It rained a right smart last night and I 'low we won't be workin' in that bottom ground for a few days." I merely nodded because Jake was deaf. He was a dowser, using a spindly, forked branch from a tree to find water or whatever he might have lost and was looking for.

Some years later, at a family gathering, I was looking for some change which had fallen from my pocket during a rough and tumble game. Jake saw me looking and said, "I 'low I can find it." He cut a small, forked limb from a maple tree, stuck a dime in a slit on the stub end of the fork, and holding a prong of the forked limb in each hand, thumbs outward, criss-crossed the lawn. Suddenly he paused, concentrated on an area about a yard square, then bent over and picked up four or five coins. I thought there was some trick—I knew dowsers could find water, but surely not metal objects, so I wrote on a piece of paper that I was skeptical, that I wanted to see if he could do it again. He agreed and I sent him behind the house with his grandson Dennis to make sure he wasn't "peeping" and then hid a dime under a leaf. Back and forth he went, then halted again when he reached the vicinity of the dime. Suddenly, he bent over and picked it up. My skepticism was gone. Jake, pleased that I was now a true believer, said, in the monotone voice of a deaf speaker, "I lost my keys once, so I put an old key in the end of the fork and found them."

I didn't plow any more new ground for Jake that summer. Aside from new ground, I enjoyed plowing, and plowed our land after Dad went on public works. I often went barefoot and the endless stream of shiny, brown earth appeared almost liquid as it came off the silvery, well-scoured moldboard of the plow. Occasionally, I plowed out a lethargic snake, whose winter sleep was rudely interrupted, or picked up an Indian arrowhead lost by earlier users of the land.

When Dad left the farm to take up "public work," a job on a section crew for the Southern Railway maintaining track, someone had to take care of the crops he had planted that spring. I was ten or eleven years old, and not yet mature enough to do it by myself, so Dad hired Harold Gearner and me to plow the corn. Harold was a bachelor, probably forty years old, and had managed to get to that age without ever doing any steady work. Harold was a professional hobo. Every fall, when the weather turned sharp, Harold hopped a freight, and headed for a warmer climate. In the spring, he returned to Duff and sustained himself by doing odd jobs and some farm work. He also played the fiddle, which earned him many a swig from the bottle, a meal here and there, and a bed for the night. When Harold was hired, the corn was about a foot high and in need of cultivation. Dad had a walking cultivator, which was designed to have the operator walk behind and control the cultivator shovels by hand, one on either side of the row of corn. A team of horses or mules pulled the cultivator, and the operator, with his hands occupied, controlled the team by lines looped around his waist. Perhaps Dad thought Harold would stay at the job a little better if I worked with him, so he nailed a board across the twin shafts of the cultivator, and I sat on the board and drove the horses while Harold operated the shovels. We kept a jug of water buried in the dirt at the end of the row, and had to give the horses a rest after every couple of rounds. After a refreshing drink of water, we sat in the shade and with some prompting, Harold told me about life on the road. Truth is, Harold might have worked harder had I not been there, as I was always causing him to return to the subject of his hobo experiences.

My pay was twenty-five cents a day—I don't know how much Dad paid Harold, but it was probably the going rate of one dollar a day. At the end of the week, I had earned a dollar and twenty-five cents and was thinking of all the ways I was going to spend it. On Saturday, Dad suggested that he and I should go to Charlie Spurlock's store. I had not yet received my pay but was certain I would be paid there. When we arrived, Dad asked, "Charlie, do you have any shoes that will fit this boy? You know, something tough and a little too big—something that will hold him for a while?" I was kind of surprised because we kids went barefoot in summer to save shoe leather, and besides, we preferred going barefoot

I got the uneasy feeling that I wasn't going to be spending my pay. Uncle Charlie (who was married to Minnie Songer, my Dad's sister) said, "Yes, Hugo, I have one pair of shoes that will fit him, and they ought to do the trick." When he pulled them out, I stood there, mouth open, gaping at the ugliest pair of shoes I had ever seen. Those dandies had square toes, which was bad enough, but worse than that, they were *orange* with soles as hard as hickory wood! Unfortunately, they fit, which means they were too large, just as Dad wanted and what's more, he was impressed with their box-like construction. He bought them on the spot with my pay. I hated those shoes and continued to go barefoot all summer. I dreaded the razzing I was certain to get from schoolmates when school started.

Later that summer, I worked for Gus Ahrens in his strawberry fields. He and I and his son Carl, who was my age, hoed strawberry plants from 6:00 am to 6:00 pm. Occasionally, the long, boring days were interrupted by blessed rain, or about once a week, the arrival of the huckster wagon. We could hear him coming from a half mile away as pots and pans and other kinds of cookware banged against the wagon and each other as he jolted along the rough road. Harvey Kamman operated out of his store in Zoar and sold household wares and condiments to homesteads remote from the stores in Duff and other towns. Chickens taken in trade flapped and squawked, adding to the ruckus.

During the week, I lived with the Ahrens family, and rode my bicycle home on weekends. One summer evening after a long, hot day in the strawberry fields, Gus agreed to take us to a free show that was playing at the Duff clubhouse. All the kids were on the back of Gus's old Chevy truck and we were well on our way when the radiator boiled over, which it was wont to do. Gus always carried a bucket with which to obtain water from the nearest creek or cistern. He stopped on a small concrete bridge, which spanned a creek, and yelled for someone to grab the bucket and get some water. I volunteered, jumped off the truck, and stepped up on the small bridge abutment preparatory to jumping into the creek bed. It was a beautiful moonlit night and from my vantage point on the abutment, there appeared to be a stretch of sand four or five feet below which would make a good landing area. The full moon created an illusion from where I stood, and as I prepared to jump into the creek bed, Gus could see that it was not sand at all, but a foot or more of water. He told me later he wondered aloud, "What's that boy up to now," and tried to warn me, but his warning came too late, and I landed in a foot and a half of water and mud with my orange shoes on. They were ruined, and although Dad swore I had jumped intentionally, I continue to maintain to this day that I saw a sandbar from the bridge abutment on that moonlit night.

At some point I worked and lived with the Edwin Small family where I was paid nine dollars per week. We got up just before daylight, and went immediately to the barn to feed and harness the horses. Then we returned to the house for a huge breakfast of eggs, bacon and ham, gravy and hot biscuits, prepared by Edwin's mother Louise and his wife Virginia. When it came time to put up hay, Edwin assembled a crew consisting of Ed Ermert, Herman Small, Edwin's cousin and neighbor, and myself, and we spent a week putting up hay. It was red clover, which grows about four feet high. The men stayed on the ground, picking up windrows of hay with pitchforks, throwing it on the hay wagon while I was on the wagon building the load. Due to the length of the hay, I could and did build huge loads. After we were loaded and the boom pole was in place, I drove the horses, which strained under the load, toward the barn. As I approached the barnyard gate, it appeared that the width of the load was at least as wide as the gateway. Edwin yelled up at me, "Be careful and don't knock down one of those gateposts." I had an excellent vantage point from the top of the load, as I stood there straddling the boompole eight feet above the horses. I carefully drove the load exactly in the center of the gateway and knocked down both gateposts!

Later that summer, I worked for Herman Small. I had taken a team of horses, a mower, a jug of water and my lunch to his river bottoms to mow a hay field. Late in the afternoon, just as I had reduced the field of hay to a small triangular patch, I mowed through a huge bumblebee nest. Bumblebees nest in the ground, and it was impossible to see the nest in the tall grass. Suddenly, hundreds of bees were swarming around the horses and me, stinging the horses, causing them to rear and step over the tongue of the mower and get entangled in each other's harness. By surprise and shock, rather than by intention, I sat very still on the mower seat and did not get stung. The attack continued for several minutes, as the bumblebees swarmed like small fighter planes, and was called off only after their ammunition, their stingers, were exhausted.

WAYNE HALL'S STORE

Wayne Hall's Store was the main headquarters for loafing for us boys, and if nothing was happening there, we would go up the alley to Charlie Spurlock's store, which had its regulars too: mostly men engaged in card games. Wayne's store building, located on the northwest corner of Duff, was considerably dilapidated, but it had a false front, which gave it a look of importance.

A large sales room in front contained general merchandise. Shelves filled with canned goods lined the north wall from floor to ceiling, except that the top shelves held larger, less-often purchased items such as chamber pots, coal buckets, and pails. On the south wall were soft goods such as underwear and overalls. Waist-high tables held display cases, one containing candy, another school supplies, and yet another over the counter medicine such as Doan's Little Liver Pills and liniment, Lydia Pinkham's pills, and Castor Oil, a laxative all children hated.

An icebox in the back of the room, powered by a generator, cooled soft drinks, bologna and cheese. A section of the icebox kept the brick ice cream frozen. For a dime, Wayne would set you up with a slab of ring bologna, mustard, crackers, and a soft drink. A smaller lower room in the back contained coal oil (kerosene), animal feed, and the gen-erator. Near the back of the main room was a large cannonball coal stove surrounded by church-type pews and benches for the loafers. It was always dark in the store, because its only windows were on each side of the front door.

After Wayne bought the generator, a couple of bare light bulbs, suspended on cords from the ceiling, provided additional light, but it was still dim in there. On the front porch, benches with their backs to the wall on each side of the door, and boards nailed between the porch posts, served the loafers.

Wayne Hall's store on Sunday; girls' day.

Loafin', Wayne Hall's store porch; Child, Gene Stapleton, Marvin Stapleton on bench, back to camera; standing, Leon (Pard) Heowener.

Ben Gearner, regular loafer, Wayne Hall's store.

E. Wayne Hall, Store Keeper.

Hugo E. Songer, with daughters Judy, Janice, and Mary Ann on Wayne Hall's store porch.

The front door, which appeared ancient, as if it had been swinging on its hinges for a hundred years or more, caused a bell to ring, so that Wayne would know a customer had entered if he was in the house. At the south corner of the store porch stood a Standard gasoline pump: the kind with a glass container at the top of which the gallons, from one to ten, were marked. Gasoline was pumped into the glass tank with a hand-powered pump and it flowed into the automobile gas tank by gravity. At twenty cents a gallon, the customary purchase was one dollar. Mounted on the front wall of the store on either side of the windows, were metal signs that advertised various products such as "Orange Crush 5 cents" or "Smoke Model Tobacco."

Wayne must have been Duff's storekeeper for thirty years or more, and I knew him only as an old man. He was lanky, with thinning hair and a hawk nose, and was somewhat stooped. Most importantly, he had a great disposition. If he was asked to open the store on Sunday afternoon when he was ordinarily closed so that you could purchase some emergency item, just to let you know it was an imposition, he said "Doggone," and continued mumbling as he led you through the short hallway between his house and the store. In summer, when the loafers gathered on the front porch, Wayne remained inside, sitting on one of the benches, napping and nodding, with a drop of sweat at the end of his nose.

There were a number of regulars, including Ben Gearner, a tattooed, pensioned Navy veteran who had served in the Boxer Rebellion in China, and who claimed to have walked on the China Wall. Ben roomed at his Aunt Nan Summers' house, and at the end of the month when his pension check arrived, Ben paid his store bill and rent, and laid in a month's supply of pipe tobacco. He'd gather a couple of drinking buddies and call Bennie Green's taxi service for a ride to Huntingburg, where he went for a binge that lasted as long as his pension check, then back to Duff and the store porch, roaring drunk.

The boys got on Ben pretty hard when he was drinking, knowing that he would be easily provoked. We accused him of lying about the China Wall, and wondered out loud whether he had even been in China, or for that matter, in the Navy. He was a creative "cusser" and let fly a string of swear words, waved his cane in the air, and threatened to whack "every one of you little sons-a-bitches."

Ben was street-wise, and there is no question but that he had whored and binged in many an Oriental port. He was crippled, allegedly from the ravages of a dread disease he had picked up in an Asian brothel. No matter what time of day you went to Wayne's store, you could be sure of a conversation with Ben Gearner.

Another regular, Hugo Lemond, had inherited a large farm from his father, and performed very little labor himself, so he had plenty of time for the store porch. He had a substantial girth, and due to his obesity, about the only manual labor he could perform was to crawl up on the seat of his old Fordson tractor and work the fields. He kept an elderly hired hand named Loney whose pay consisted of room and board and tobacco money. Hugo hired boys on the store porch, paid them the least he could, and even then, made them wait for their meager pay until he sold farm products on the excuse that he would have no money until then. He was a friendly man, likeable, and in some ways generous—the baseball diamond was in his pasture field across the road from Wayne Hall's store. Hugo, more well read than most of the other Duffers, was always pontificating on war and rumors of war. Other daytime loafers were the old men, those who were laid off, farmers who stopped by, and the young boys. Sometimes the ladies lingered a while too, particularly those who needed a respite after walking a mile or two to get there.

In winter, when we sat around the pot-bellied stove with a cold rain falling outside, there was a reluctance to leave the rosy glow of the stove and the company gathered there. The story tellers, aware they had a captive audience, often launched into a story of a past experience, or some tall tale. A farmer would enter, stomp the mud or snow off his boots, and begin a narrative about rescuing a cow experiencing a difficult delivery, a sick horse, or a runaway.

In the left corner of the store as you entered was a six-by-six-foot cage that served as the post office. Mail came in on the noon train, old #24, and if passengers got off, the mailbag was placed on the depot platform. Otherwise, the train didn't stop and the heavy canvas mailbag was thrown off on the run. Sometimes the bag tumbled onto the platform, and sometimes it slid off into a deep ditch of rocks and weeds. Wayne, who had gone to meet the train with his old wooden wheelbarrow, grumbled all the way back to the store about the dog-gone train crew.

Tillie, Wayne's fiery, red-haired wife, was Duff's postmistress. Tillie's nerves were always frazzled, and it took very little to frazzle them even more. Her frizzy hair looked as if she had just stuck her finger into a light socket. She sorted the mail, placed the letters into small cubicles tabbed with the first letter of the person's name. When I was eight years old, Mom sent me to Wayne's store to get the mail. She had been expecting something from Montgomery Ward. After Tillie finished sorting, I asked for the Songers' mail. Without looking up, Tillie responded, "You're too young to get the mail." I returned home and told Mom what Tillie said. "Let's go see Tillie," she said, so we walked back to the store. Mom confronted her and said, "Tillie, this boy is eight year's old. He is very smart and responsible, and I want you to let him pick up our mail." Tillie, her dander up, said, "I don't care; he's too young to get the mail." Wayne, who had been listening to the discussion, said, "Doggone it Tillie, it's their mail. Let Charlie pick it up." Tillie reluctantly agreed, but seemed, generally, to have a proprietary interest in everyone's mail. Often, after she finished sorting, she walked away as if she didn't know we were standing there waiting. I'd say, "Tillie, I would like to get the Songers' mail." She'd respond irritably, "You don't have any mail." I could see it right there in the little box, and insisted that we did. Tillie, her face as red as her hair, nerves beginning to unravel, would return and reluctantly hand it over. There was a period when Tillie was handing out mail to the wrong people. Someone complained to the Postal Inspector, who chewed her out and made her mad. Until her nerves fell back into place, she made people call out their names when they asked for mail, even though she had known them for twenty years.

Sometimes, she waited on customers, shuffling around the store in her old blue house shoes. If a female came in and asked for some unmentionable, such as cotton panties, or long stockings, Wayne called on Tillie to serve the customer, while the boys snickered by the stove. When Wayne was away picking up produce, Tillie was in charge. A favorite section was the candy counter, and if I took too long in making up my mind, red-headed Tillie would get all fired up and tell me to make up my mind or else. It was better to buy candy at Charlie Spurlock's store anyway, because for a nickel, he filled the sack!

Wayne was an enterprising businessman, but once in a while his arithmetic got off kilter. Gobby Collins walked into his store one morning as Wayne swept out yesterday's dirt and Gobby noticed a fresh case of strawberries sitting on the counter:

> *"How much for the strawberries, Uncle Wayne?" asked his nephew Gobby. "Twelve cents a quart or two for a quarter" Wayne responded. "You mean thirteen cents a quart, don't you?" "No", he said firmly. "It's twelve cents a quart or two for a quarter." "Well," Gobby rejoined, I'll buy one quart for twelve cents, and then turn around and buy another quart for twelve cents, and I'll save a penny." "No you won't, doggonit," said Wayne, "for I know who you are, and that you have already bought a quart, and young man, you'll pay thirteen cents for that second quart—just like I said. I'm trying to give folks a break that want just a quart, and if you are too doggone dumb to understand that, you ain't got much sense!" Gobby bought a quart and went on home, secure in the knowledge he had saved a penny anyway.*

Wayne put up with a lot from the boys. If we got too wild, he called us down. We knew how far we could go. No fighting or scuffling was allowed in the store. One day Jiggs Maxey came in looking for Buck Heowener, who was sitting on a bench nearest the door. Both boys were about my age, Buck a little older. Jiggs was in a rage over something Buck had said, and called Buck every name he could think of and dared him to fight. Wayne insisted, in accordance with his house rule, that the matter be taken up outside. Jiggs kept name calling—on and on.

Finally Buck realized Jiggs was not going to stop taunting him and in order to save face, he had to fight him. Jiggs headed for the door ahead of Buck, and just as Jiggs crossed the threshold, Buck rabbit-punched him in the back of the head, and Jiggs sprawled across the porch and into the road. He recovered quickly, and the fight was on. They fought in the road, in the ditch across the road, back on the road, on the porch, and then back on the road until they were both too tired to fight anymore.

They had done considerable damage to each other—each had cuts, scrapes, bruises, and a bloody nose. The violence of the fight surprised me. Jiggs was muscular, athletic, and a fighter. In retrospect, I'm surprised he and I never fought, because we were very competitive, especially in baseball. I had scuffles with the boys, but brawls like the one Buck and Jiggs engaged in never made much sense to me. That is the reason we never fought. Jiggs, at age fifteen, used his older brother's birth certificate, enlisted in the Marines, and I haven't seen him since.

A sparrow flew into the store one day and flitted around among the chamber pots and coal buckets stored on the top shelves. Wayne was amused and tolerated it for a while, but when he realized the sparrow could not find the open door, he said, "Doggone, boys, grab some of them brooms and chase that spatsy out." Well, Buck really got into the chase and became so single-minded about getting the bird out that he seemed unaware that he was doing more damage to the merchandise than the bird could do in a year. Chamber pots and coal buckets tumbled from the shelves. Finally, Wayne was able to get Buck's attention and got him stopped. The bird escaped on its own.

The swapping of guns, knives and other doodads went on constantly. If it was hunting season, the boys usually carried long guns—shotguns or rifles. Even if hunting season wasn't in, they would bring them in to swap. None of us ever had a handgun, but Wayne did, and every once in awhile, we would persuade him to bring it out so we could hold it, aim it, and admire it. One day I was in the store alone with my old single barrel sixteen-gauge shotgun, when Wayne asked to see it. He looked it over and said, "Doggone it Charlie, I believe a shotgun would serve me better than my pistol. Tell you what I'll do. I'll swap you even." Well, I was in shock and said something like: "You mean you'll trade your beautiful pistol for my old polkstalk?" which wasn't a very smart response to someone who has just made you the offer of a lifetime. "That's right," he said, and we exchanged guns then and there. I still have that little blue steel beauty—a Smith and Wesson .32 Special.

We had no telephone at home, and on the rare occasion when we had to make a call, we used Wayne's telephone. It consisted of a large, elongated, wooden box attached to the wall. The receiver, attached to the box by a cord, reposed in a cradle on the left side of the box and the act of lifting the earpiece "turned on" the telephone. On the right side of the box was a crank, which the caller used to ring up a particular residence and the mouthpiece into which one spoke jutted out like an inverted horn from the front of the box. Wayne was on a party line along with ten other subscribers, each of whom was assigned a certain signal, such as two shorts and a long, three shorts, two longs and a short, etc. In order to ring someone up on the party line, you turned the crank, which actually turned a small electric generator in the box, to correspond to the signal of the household you wanted to reach. The problem was, when someone on the party line was called, every telephone on the party line rang. Theoretically, you were supposed to answer the telephone only if your signal was rung, but the temptation was too great in those lonely, isolated households and the someone would say, "Oh look, there is Annie Stapleton's ring; I wonder who it is and what they are calling about."

They would gently raise the receiver, and listen in. There was a series of clicks as several households tuned in to the conversation, and the line got weaker and weaker as each receiver was raised. Sometimes, a listener could not bear to stay out of the conversation when they had something to contribute or when they had failed to hear some choice bit of news. I rang up Harold Hilgeman from Wayne's store one evening to ask about baseball practice. Harold didn't know, but Frank Lowe, the manager, joined the conversation from his home and filled us in on the details.

On a cold winter day, when an icy wind whistled around the corner of the old store building and rattled the front door, men and boys filled the benches around the stove. Wayne would go to the back room and grab a big chunk of coal to feed the fire in the old cannon ball stove. The fire flared up and the wave of warmth from the stove and the fellowship of those around it caused us to hope that the afternoon would never end. My friend Gordon Hochmeister, caught the essence of Wayne Hall's store in a poem he wrote:

The ev'ning air was lettuce crisp
My ragged shirt not warm enough
I walked along and kicked at rocks
On the lonely road that led to Duff.

Once there and with the local boys
All finished with our ev'ning chore
To entertain we'd gather on
The porch in front of Wayne Hall's store

We'd tease and laugh and tell tall tales
Then walk across the oil-drenched floor
To take our place on church-type pews
Round the pot-bellied stove at Wayne Hall's Store

Dufftown

The fire a'cracklin'—a spread of warmth
With list'ning ears we'd hope for more
To learn things made for memories
Round that pot-bellied stove
at Wayne Hall's Store

BUCK HEOWENER

Buck was my second cousin—his grandmother Elmina Bailey was the sister of my grandfather, James Songer. Buck was sandy-haired, jug-eared, and had inherited the Songer nose. I liked Buck because he was willing to try anything and because he thought life and people were amusing. Buck sometimes did things to attract attention, but he needn't have. He was clearly eccentric for a boy his age. He might come to school in the dead of winter wearing short sleeves and in the heat of summer, a sheepskin coat. At the stores, he was at the center of many escapades. He accepted bets that he could do things, like eat five pounds of bologna at a sitting.

We were having lunch at Wayne's store—bologna and cheese, crackers and mustard, when Buck said: "Man, this bologna is good. I bet I could eat five pounds of it." I said, "Oh, come on Buck, the bologna's good all right, but you can't eat five pounds." The other guys chimed in and ridiculed Buck's claim and soon the bet was on. Wayne cut a five-pound slab of bologna and plunked it down in the middle of an oilcloth-covered table. Buck relished the first two pounds, slowed down on the third, belched his way through the fourth, then nibbled away at the fifth for over an hour before downing the last bite. He won the bet so we had to chip in and pay Wayne for the bologna. Another time, he bet he could drink ten Pepsis in an hour, and on the eighth bottle, he bolted from the store to vomit in order to make room for the remaining two bottles. We argued for a while over whether this was permitted, but it hadn't been mentioned when we made the bet, so we paid off. I suspect Buck took this behavior from his Dad, who once bet the clay miners he could carry a live one hundred pound hog on his back for a mile, and won. If we were going fishing, hunting, swimming, halloweening, or were otherwise up to no good, Buck was sure to be there.

He was not a good student, hated school, and was always getting in trouble. The teacher, Sophia Arensman, who was patient with Buck, was the only person in the world who called him by his given name, which was Henry Edgar. Buck seriously tried Miss Arensman's patience in many different ways. Sometimes, he let out tremendous farts. He was on of those unusual people who could fart at will. Miss Arensman, an old maid schoolteacher who couldn't bear to say the word, glared at Buck and said, "Henry Edgar, you may stop making those unnecessary noises!" Early one spring day, Buck came to school with his clothing saturated with skunk spray. He sat close to the stove and soon the odor of skunk filled the one room school with an overwhelming stench. I was watching Sophia's increasing discomfort and suddenly, she stomped her foot and said, "Henry Edgar, you may leave and don't come back until the skunk odor is gone." Buck was out of school for a week. Another of Buck's deficits was sports. He was strong, but uncoordinated. Every year, toward the end of school, Duff school played Warnsman School in a baseball game. Buck and I were the only 8th graders, and there was a scarcity of larger boys who could also play baseball. We talked it over and decided we had no other choice—I would pitch and Buck would catch. We borrowed the catcher's equipment from the Duff Indians and, on the appointed day, Buck put it on—mask, chest protector, and shin guards. Our schoolyard games were played with a rubber ball, but for this game we used a real baseball, and I could throw hard. Buck caught the baseball only a few times that day, and those were occasions when the baseball kind of wandered into his glove. The rest of the time, if the Warnsman boys didn't hit it, the baseball went past him or hit him, sometimes on the mask or chest and sometimes on an unprotected area. I winced every time he got hit and fully expected him to tear off the equipment and leave, but Buck was game and stuck it out, his body containing many round, blue bruises for several days.

Buck's speech was laced with swear words. For this and other reasons, my Mom did not like for me to pal around with him. She always said he cussed too much, but it wasn't that, because I didn't need a better teacher than Dad. I think she was concerned I would get into trouble if I was around Buck. But Buck and I got together often. One day we were squirrel hunting in Uncle Jake's woods. We knew Jake's bull had the run of that woods, so we kept an eye out for him. I shot a squirrel which lodged in a fork, and was circling the tree looking for a clear shot. Sometimes you could shoot them out when they hung up.

Suddenly, I saw the bull top the hill and head in my direction. I decided to cross the fence only a few yards away, and had swung a leg across when I heard Buck's double-barreled shotgun go off. I turned in time to see the bull jump, turn tail in midair, and run bellowing over the hill from whence he came. Buck had shot the bull in the rear with both barrels from about seventy-five yards, claiming that he had saved my life. Years later, I ran into Buck as he was making the rounds of local bars dressed as a mountain man. He asked, "Charles, do you remember when I shot Jake's bull?" I said, "Buck, how could I forget!" and Buck replied, "You wouldn't be standing here today if I hadn't shot that bull. I ran into your mother the other day and told her how I saved your life." Then he grinned and said: "You know, I've been shootin' the bull ever since."

Later, when I returned to this area, I learned that Buck was in the hospital in poor shape. I visited him there, and indeed found him that way. His doctor told me that Buck was admitted with acute alcoholism, including delirium tremens, and that his prognosis was extremely poor due to the damage to his liver. He said that if Buck ever started drinking again, it would kill him. Buck needed to go to a nursing home for a few weeks, he continued, and needed a guardian. None of his family wanted to be guardian, with good reason, because Buck was tough to handle.

I began visiting him in the nursing home, and toward the end of his stay, agreed to be his guardian. Upon his release from the nursing home, we rented a house trailer for him and shopped for the necessary towels, sheets, groceries, etc. to get him started at housekeeping. He had income, a railroad disability pension, resulting from injuries he received when he fell from a bridge. Buck began talking about the place where he had lived before he was hospitalized, saying that he had personal effects and about fifteen guns there. I could also tell that he was apprehensive about returning there. But he wanted his guns, so we drove to the site of another house trailer and a large and very angry woman threw open the door. It turns out Buck had been her meal ticket when he lived there and as part of the arrangement, she supplied him with whiskey, and their living expenses were paid for with Buck's railroad disability pension. She was mad because Buck had left, and was going to keep the guns, she said, as compensation for allowing Buck to stay there. I puffed up, brushed past her, and found Buck's guns in a small closet. I swooped them up and we were out of there amid threats of being sued for trespass and theft.

After a few weeks, Buck said he wanted to visit the nursing home he had left. He had never mentioned before that he had become close friends with a female patient. About once a week, we went to the nursing home so they could visit. Surprisingly, Buck's health continued to improve and one day he said he and his friend wanted to get married. I was definitely not in favor of this, because Buck had been married three times before and clearly had difficulty with relationships. But his mind was made up and inasmuch as I had recently been elected judge, I married them at the trailer. I felt the guardianship should end now that Buck had a wife, so it was ended and Buck was no longer my ward.

I dropped in for a visit after a couple of weeks and things seemed to be going along fairly well, but as several weeks passed, it became clear that wedded bliss had not settled in at Buck's trailer. One day, I dropped by unannounced, and there was a half gallon of whiskey on the table. Buck was drinking again. I told Buck he might as well be playing with dynamite, but he denied drinking while we sat there with the bottle between us. Also, I noticed that Buck's guns were disappearing one by one. He was selling or giving them away to young boys in the trailer court, or more likely, they were stealing them. About this time, Buck's wife left and he got a divorce, and shortly after that, was married again, but he didn't stop drinking. Soon, he was again hospitalized with a diagnosis of cancer. This time he did not leave the hospital. Buck was dead, and a large part of my living connection with old Duff died also.

THE CHICKEN YARD

One bright, cold November morning, Jiggs Maxey, Buck Heowener and I were in Wayne's store discussing what a perfect day it was for rabbit hunting. Perfect, because it had frozen the night before and the dogs' noses worked much better on a cold day. My uncle Vern Woodruff had left two beagle hounds with me to take care of that fall. Their names were Red and Dukey Doo, whom I called Driver. Red, the older dog, was a wonderful tracker with a real nose for rabbits. He worked slowly and always stayed on the trail, while Driver ran too fast and lost the trail, requiring him to backtrack. Red worked almost silently, but Driver had a beautiful voice and used it frequently. When they had a rabbit going in one of those hollows on the Utz or Fenneman place, it was pure joy to sit on the side of a hill and listen and watch them work. That fall and winter I was very popular with the other boys who liked rabbit hunting behind Red and Driver.

Just as we were ready to leave to get our guns and the dogs, a local farmer, McCullough, rolled up in his 1932 Chevy. He asked the three of us to work for him that day. His corn had been cut and shocked and he wanted us to take his mules and wagon, tear the shocks apart and shuck the corn, and haul it to his granary. There was an unwritten rule that you could evade someone who wanted you to work, but if you were "caught" and asked to work, unless you had a good excuse, you couldn't refuse. McCullough caught us fair and square so we had to go to work for him. There is an old saying that when you hire a boy to work, you've hired a boy; when you have hired two boys, you've hired half a boy; and when you have hired three boys, you have hired no boys at all. But that was McCullough's problem, so we piled into his Plymouth and headed for his farm.

McCullough was a notoriously hard drinker and his drink of

choice was peach brandy. He was also known to become violent when he was drinking, which was most of the time. It was clear that on this day, he had been hitting the bottle pretty hard. We hitched up the mules to the box wagon, drove to the cornfield, and began shucking corn from the shocks, all the while lamenting the loss of a rabbit hunt on this beautiful November day. Also, there was ice in the shocks and none of us wore gloves. Jiggs was the first one to complain, and soon we all joined in.

On the way to the barn with the third load, we decided to quit work and go rabbit hunting. With some apprehension, we approached McCullough's front door. It was agreed that Jiggs would knock and I would announce that we were quitting. Jiggs knocked and I said, "Mr. McCullough, our hands are cold and we are quitting"—failing to mention our intended rabbit hunt. There was a pause and then I heard a rattling sound like he was getting a gun from behind a cabinet and at the same time I thought I heard him say, "If you sons-a-bitches come in here I'm gonna kill all of you." I turned quickly to the other two guys and said: "Did you hear what I heard?"

Clearly they had for without a word, they turned and ran a blue streak for the yard gate which was near the southwest corner of the yard and on the south side. Also near the southwest corner of the yard but on the west side of the yard fence was a gateway to the chicken yard. I saw Buck open the wrong gate and I yelled at him, but it was too late and as I was running across the barn lot, I looked over my shoulder and saw Buck make a full circle of the chicken yard, chickens squawking and flying in every direction, some flying over the ten foot fence for the first time in their lives and one rooster even seeking refuge on Buck's head for a few strides. After a full tour of the chicken yard, Buck found the right gate and joined Jiggs and me who were waiting for him around the corner of the barn.

We ran cross country for a half mile or so and then worked our way to the road that ran toward Duff. Just as we found ourselves in a cut (high banks on each side) in the rock road, McCullough came roaring over the hill in his Chevy. Frantically, we scrambled up the bank to make our escape and did not return to the road for the remainder of our trek to Duff. Jiggs and I were willing to let the matter rest there, but Buck's Dad called the sheriff and told him what had happened. Later, the sheriff came to Duff, asked a few questions, talked to McCullough, and so far as I know, had a peach brandy with him, and that was the end of it. That same afternoon, Buck, Jiggs, and I sat on a hillside overlooking Fenneman holler, reliving the events of the morning, laughing about Buck's tour of the chicken yard, and listening to the bugle voice of Driver as he and Red, hot on the trail of a rabbit, wove their way through the briar-filled thickets, the same ones where our family had picked blackberries that summer.

THE RAILROAD

The railroad played a central role in almost every aspect of our lives. After all, Duff had been "transplanted" from old Dufftown, located one mile south, to be near the railroad. A freight, called the Local, delivered fencing, tires, stoves, and other hardware to every whistle-stop, including Duff. The westbound passenger train, called #24, dropped off and picked up passengers and the eastbound evening train, #23, did the same.

I was fascinated by the green steam engines that pulled the passenger trains, with their great six-feet-tall driving wheels, built for speed. The depot platform was not very wide—certainly not more than eight feet, so even with my back pressed against the railing, I was still reasonably close to the tracks. When that great engine pulled in, its bell ringing, steam coming from every pore, its silvery, steel arm slashing the air, it was like some green metallic monster making a daily visit. As soon as the passengers boarded or got off, two quick toots of the whistle indicated the train was about to leave the station. More often than not, when the train pulled out, the driver wheels spun on the steel rails, and there was a great gushing of steam and smoke. As she approached Steineker crossing, the rising and falling tones of her whistle echoed across the hills and valleys surrounding Duff and I concluded that life was good.

Many Duffers worked on the railroad. Two were employed as telegraphers, at least a half dozen as engineers and firemen on the steam engines, and easily that number worked on the section gang repairing track. Most of the "runs" for the crewmen were between St. Louis and Louisville. The engineers became artists with the steam whistles, and each developed his own distinctive style. When they pulled their trains through Duff, they heralded their approach with their signature whistle, and people would pause at their tasks and say,

Southern Railway Freight Train.

Duff Depot, looking west.

Wayne Hall's garage, on left; Duff Crossing, looking south.

"There goes Chris, or Lem, or Lawrence." Late at night, when I heard the mournful tones of the whistle, I experienced great comfort and happiness in knowing that one of the Duff boys was pulling her by.

Four of the Small brothers, Charlie, Chris, Lem, and Frank, were engineers. They had been inspired to become railroaders by their Uncle Lem, who had learned to operate the early steam engines used on farms, and when the railroad was built, got a job operating the steam engines that ran on rails. Lemuel said that when his uncle came by the Small farm, he threw apples to him and had to learn to throw the apple ahead of the onrushing engine, so that the apple fell into the waiting hands of Uncle Lem as he roared by. The Small boys were cousins and close friends of my dad. He and Lem and Chris, in particular, got together hundreds of times over the years, and every occasion was marked by drinking (often home brew) and singing, mostly railroad songs. In summer, they often partied on our screened-in porch. Tying binder twine to the necks of the quart bottles of home brew, they lowered them into a deep cistern located under the porch to cool the beer. "You know," Lemuel would say, "the Bible says drinking is okay," and he would quote the Scripture "a little wine for thine stomach's sake and thine ofttimes infirmities."

The romance of "workin' on the railroad" was always very personal to us. After Dad died, Lem and I continued to be good friends. Once, I asked Lem's wife Eloise what it was like to be a railroader's wife. She said, "Listen," in her sassy way of speaking, "I was a railroader's daughter before I was a railroader's wife. Around our household, the rule was that you had to answer the telephone by the end of the second ring. Someone in the family had to be within earshot of the telephone twenty-four hours a day." She explained that many times the men were on call and didn't know when they would be asked to make a run. Sometimes, they were asleep, having finished a run only a few hours before. If they didn't answer the phone by the third ring, the dispatcher might hang up and call someone else. Her Dad, "Legs" Wilson, was an engineer. One day, the Wilson family was planning to go to a Labor Day picnic, when one of those calls came at the last

Chris and Lem Small, railroad engineers.

minute, and Legs was required to substitute for another engineer. Eloise explained, "He hated cats and would never tolerate them in the house. Mom and I thought it was peculiar when he called the cat that morning and let it in. As he prepared to leave, he said, 'One of these days one of those big hogs is gonna' step on me.' We knew that the big steam engines were sometimes called hogs, but didn't know what he meant." Later that day, east of Duff, near the town of Francisco, two trains collided head-on, and Legs Wilson was dead.

Lemuel Small was a dandy. He was quite handsome—looked like Valentino—with his black hair slicked back, dark eyes, and a cookie duster mustache. He loved singing and had his own "throw back your head and let her rip" style. His favorite song was "Carolina Moon" because his pioneer ancestors had come from North Carolina, and when he launched into that song, he crossed his legs, reared back his head, and belted it out. His pioneer accent and lilting intonations were unique and entertaining. He pronounced the word "camera" with a "y" on the end of it. Among ourselves, we joked and said, "Lem is going to take his camery to Africy and Floridy." Both Lem and Chris spoke from behind the back of their hand, as if what they were telling you was highly confidential, even though they knew, and intended, that anyone within twenty feet could hear what they were saying.

He and his brother Chris developed a patter for fellow tavern patrons. Chris might lean towards Lem and say, "I went hunting last night," and Lem would respond, "You did! Did you get any?" And Chris would reply, "Just one, that's all I can handle at one time." All the tavern patrons thought it hilarious.

Lemuel had lots of railroad stories, and he told them in that high-pitched, lilting pioneer manner. On one occasion, Lemuel related that he was firing a passenger engine which was approaching an "S" curve just out of New Albany, Indiana. "We were doing about sixty miles an hour, and as we got closer and closer to the curve, I realized that the engineer was not slowing down." At this point, Lemuel explained that an engineer is like a captain on a ship. He is in charge:

Lemuel Potter Small, railroad engineer and raconteur.

a lowly fireman just doesn't tell an engineer what to do. Finally, in desperation, Lem said, "My God man, give 'er some air!" (meaning, apply the air brakes) "But by that time, it was too late. My God, we hit the curve and the engine reared up on the outside wheels. It had just settled down when we hit the second curve and my God, the engine went up on the wheels on the other side. Screaming passengers were thrown out of their seats and luggage was strewn around the passenger cars."

As they approached the station in Louisville, and were rolling to a stop, Lemuel saw the conductor come running. Lemuel said, "I knew there was going to be Hell to pay!" So he decided to pull a preemptive strike. Before the Conductor got a word out, Lemuel shouted, "My God, that was a close one—the track on the 'S' curve is badly out of line—why, it threw the passengers out of their seats and threw their luggage around—Man, you've got to get some men over there to work on that track." What Lemuel knew was that the track would be out of line, with the engine having gone up on its wheels on one side, and that it would be impossible to prove it wasn't out of line before they went through the curve. There was an investigation, which came to naught.

When diesels began to replace the steam engines, the romance was gone, and Lemuel wanted to retire early. He explained to a sympathetic doctor that his knee was bad and he could no longer guarantee that he could keep his foot on the dead man's pedal. (The dead man's pedal was a safety device that prevented the risk of a runaway train in the event the engineer suffered a heart attack or some similar problem.) The doctor agreed that there was indeed some risk of having Lemuel continue and Lemuel retired from railroading, and for the next fifteen years, regaled us with stories and songs about the railroad. Lemuel would never agree when I asserted that working as a crewman on the great steam engines was romantic, but before he died, he had a steam engine etched into his tombstone.

Lemuel's oldest brother Charlie was a railroad engineer and a Primitive Baptist preacher. Like the other Small boys, he had a great gift of gab, and his preaching experience had enhanced it. He would launch into a mini-sermon with the slightest excuse. One beautiful July 4th afternoon, Charlie, his three brothers, and Dad and I were sitting in Lem's front yard. The conversation turned to the subject of hard times. Charlie, at least ten years older than the others, said they had never experienced times as hard as the family experienced during the depression of 1907. As Christmas approached that year, he had heard his parents, Elmer and Ellie, saying there was going to be nothing special for Christmas dinner because they had no money. At that point, Charlie launched into a sermon about all the miracles that were described in the Bible—how Moses parted the Red Sea (which was described in great detail), how Jesus raised Lazarus from the dead, and fed the multitude with five fishes (again, with much embellishment).

The "sermon" went on and on until Lemuel, who had heard the story many times, and had been fidgeting in his chair, said: "Charlie, for God's sake, get to the goose." Charlie's reverie was broken by Lem's interjection, and said, "Oh—well, Christmas morning came and I was thinking how slim the pickin's were going to be for Christmas dinner, when suddenly Mom yelled, 'Charlie, look at that big fat wild goose out there in the yard.' I looked out and sure enough, there it was. I had no trouble catching it—I just walked over and picked it up. Mom roasted the goose and we had a wonderful Christmas dinner. We thanked God for his miracle." Thereafter, in our family, when we thought someone was going into too much detail in telling their story, we would say, "Get to the goose."

Chris Small, second oldest of the Small boys, was a wonderful guy, with a sweet disposition, a warm smile, and a great sense of humor. He was also remarkably patient, particularly with his sharp-tongued wife, Doris. Perhaps he felt that he had to atone, somehow, for a terribly tragic event that occurred when he was six years old. His parents, Elmer and Ellie Small (my grandfather's sister), were faithful members of the Little Flock Primitive Baptist Church. Ellie and Brother Flener, the preacher, came to be suspected of having an affair, although the only actual evidence I have ever heard was that Ellie was seen passing Brother Flener a note.

One Day, Brother Flener was making a pastoral visit at the Small residence and Elmer learned that he was there. Brother Flener was warned of Elmer's approach with his horse and buggy, and scurried out the back door as Elmer came in the front. Elmer loaded his shotgun and gave chase but Brother Flener got away. Elmer returned to the house and placed the loaded shotgun in the corner of the kitchen. Later, young Christian, age six, picked up the shotgun, pointed it at his teen aged sister Este, said, "Bang, Bang," and pulled the trigger, and Este fell dead. Ellie (Sunderman) Borman, daughter of Andah and Mary Sunderman, who were distant neighbors of the Small family, heard the "awfullest wailing" coming from the Small residence, scurried across the fields and learned of the terrible tragedy. In the aftermath, Ellie Small was excluded from the church, and Brother Flener was fired. Elmer Small filed suit against Flener in the U.S. District court in Evansville, on the grounds of alienation of affections, but a Federal jury cleared Flener of any wrong-doing.

When business began to pick up in 1940-41, Lemuel talked Dad into getting a job on the railroad. The firemen ranks were full, so Dad had to settle for work on a section gang repairing track. It was hot, hard work in summer, with the blazing sun reflecting off the rails and ties, and in spite of the heat, men handling the creosoted cross ties wore long sleeves and overalls to avoid creosote burn. In the winter, when temperatures fell to around zero degrees, and an icy wind swept down the tracks, the foreman allowed the men to warm up around cross tie fires. Dad was a hard worker, and on the farm, he had always been his own boss. He was very sensitive to criticism, and when he felt the foreman was being unfair or patronizing, Dad was likely to rebel. Once, several cars derailed on a curve west of Duff, near Velpen, and Dad's crew was assigned to work the wreck. A carload of beer had left the rails and was lying on its side. Forrest Cooper, the foreman, called the men together and said, "Men, we have to get this wreck cleaned up and clear the track so the company can get the trains running again. As most of you know by now, there is a car load of beer over there, and I will fire the first son-of-a-bitch I catch in that beer car."

They had worked about twelve hours when some of the crewmen realized they hadn't seen Hugo for a while. They looked about and one of them saw a beer bottle come flying out of the boxcar they had all been warned about. By this time, Forrest Cooper had caught onto Hugo's absence and when he looked in the boxcar door, there was Hugo, surrounded by beer, jerking off the caps on a nail driven into the side of the boxcar. Forrest had to keep his word and fired him, although he told him later in the day he hated to do it. He even offered him the job back, but Dad refused, and missed earning a railroad pension by less than a year. Funny thing, he never seemed to have any regret about such missed opportunities.

In 1968, long after I had left Duff, a friend of mine from Evansville, who had been a reporter for the *Chicago Tribune* brought me a clipping from that paper which said simply: "Eleven Southern railroad cars derailed on a curve east of Duff, Indiana, yesterday." That same day, I hurried to Duff to see the wreck. Some of the cars were empty, and others were loaded with a variety of merchandise. The car that caught the Duffers' attention was loaded with work gloves, with the brand name, "Green Apes." So, Duffers began a *salvage* operation and soon the carload of "Green Apes" was liberated. I managed to find a few of them and upon my return to Evansville, bundled up a pair and sent then to my friend, Noel Peltier, with a note that they were a gift from the people of Duff. He sent his thanks in a letter as follows:

My Dear Commissioner:

I was deeply touched yesterday upon receiving a memento from the municipality of Duff, Indiana. It was particularly meaningful knowing that it had been inspired by one of that city's most illustrious sons. It shall take its place in my remembrance case along with the pair of fuscia socks and drabplum colored tie which have been graciously bestowed upon me in the past. However, this has far more meaning than just a small material thing in one's showcase of memories.

As you know, I have been concerned for some time that the City of Duff was not receiving its true recognition for the part it has played in the development of American culture, science and industry. Few know how the works of Plato, Aristotle, and Socrates have been devoured within this cultural center by the citizens as they sat perched upon their frigid pedestals of outdoor plumbing.

When I first heard of this unfortunate wreck by the Southern Railway Company, I was disturbed that the city would be henceforth known for the "Rape of the Freight's Green Apes;" but these gloves, carefully preserved by the citizenry, demonstrate again that Duff will continue to achieve the greatness to which it is destined.

I would like to suggest that we take the initiative and erect in a central location within the city a living memorial to how culture persevered over adversity in this great year. Perhaps we could have crossed green gloves mounted above a perpetual torch with the words appropriately inscribed below:

The sovereignty of Duff,
where hearts and hands are warm
and gloves are hot.

Yes, the railroad provided much of the employment, excitement, romance, trauma and humor for the people of Duff.

When the railroad was built in 1881, the construction crew was required to cut through Steineker Hill a mile west of Duff. The cut exposed a strata of clay five feet thick. In 1927, the P. Bannon Pipe Company of Louisville, Kentucky, decided to mine it for use in manufacturing sewer pipe. Its manager came to Duff on the train and stopped at Spurlock's store. People were impressed with this well dressed man and wondered what he wanted. He quickly satisfied their curiosity and announced that he was opening a clay mine in the area and needed a manager. Charlie Spurlock said, "There's your man," and pointed to Jake Songer, another of my grandpa's brothers. The man hired Jake on the spot and suddenly, Jake Songer became an important man in the community.

Economic activity picked up—the pipe company purchased several hundred acres surrounding Steineker Hill, and men were hired to build a tipple and cut mine props to hold up the overburden. Soon, miners were hired and a shaft was driven into the hill. The hourly rate was thirty cents, and after six hard days work, the payroll check was fourteen dollars and forty cents. Typically, eight to ten men worked the mine, so the total payroll was in excess of one hundred dollars a week and suddenly, a reasonable amount of prosperity hit Duff. Jake never got rich, paying himself only twenty dollars per week, but after assuming the manager's role, he dressed the part, always wearing a suit and tie with a gold watch chain across his expansive middle.

The men gathered at the depot in the morning and walked a mile along the railroad tracks to the mine. They wore miner's caps with an attachment on the front to accommodate the carbide lamp. Each miner had a separate room off the main shaft where he set his dynamite charges in the clay wall, and after the clay was blasted loose, he shoveled it into a small car approximately 4 by 5 and 3 feet deep. Rails had been laid to various rooms, and as they probed deeper into the hill, the track was extended. When a car was full, another miner would hitch a mine mule to the car and pull it to the tipple.

The mine mules were kept on the Steineker farm on top of the hill. Uncle Jake came to own the Steineker place, and he loved those diminutive mules, always making sure they were well fed and watered. At the end of the tipple, which extended several feet above a railroad car on a siding below, was a turntable. The mules were trained to make the turn instead of plunging off the end of the tipple. The ends of the mine car were switched on the turntable and the car was pushed the last few feet to a point where the rails were bent into a U shape to hold the car when the platform on which the car sat was tipped and the contents dumped into a railroad car on the siding below. About twenty-five mine-car loads were required to fill a railroad car. The mine crew loaded a railroad car per day until the Depression, when demand fell and only a couple of cars a week were needed.

After Franklin Roosevelt was elected President, and his works projects were enacted into law, demand picked up again as local governmental units in the Midwest engaged in projects which used clay products, especially sewer pipe. As a result, employment remained fairly good at the clay mine during the Depression, and the town of Duff continued to enjoy the weekly payroll in excess of one hundred dollars. Uncle Jake hired laid-off railroaders, and when the railroad requested they make an occasional run, he allowed them to take off work at the mine in order to make their run.

Uncle Jake's entire record-keeping system was a "Time Book" which fit into his shirt pocket, where he recorded the hours worked by each man, and expenses, such as amounts paid to Ed Ermert for mule shoes or the repair of a mine car, or the purchase of dynamite and carbide for the miner's lamps. During the twelve years he kept those books, he rarely made gratuitous comments. In fact, he made them so rarely that one would have to assume only the most important events in his life deserved mention. They were as follows:

James M. Songer died on June 10, 1934, Sunday at 4:00 AM
Drought broke up on June 30, 1936
Mother [Mary Ann] past away July 11, 1936, at 7:30 PM
Boys struck for more money March 20, 1937.
Want $3.00 per day, compromised on $2.70.
Henry Borman hurt by Mule who sat down on him Nov. 14, 1938, at 10:00 AM
Thomas Songer [his brother] hurt on Tipple at 9:30 AM July 18, 1939

George, the mine mule, died Feb 8, 1941, at 2:00 PM on the Steineker Farm.

THE DRIVERS

The old men were terrible drivers. This wasn't a young man's prejudice against the old—they really were inept. They had grown up in horse and buggy days and arrived at middle age before the new-fangled machines came along. They were, so to speak, too old to learn. Take Uncle Tom for example, who was born in 1882. Uncle Tom learned to drive a Model T but never left the horse and buggy behind. The Model T had gas and magneto levers on either side of the steering column. The magneto lever controlled the amount of spark and the gas lever the amount of gas. Both had to be pulled simultaneously to provide the engine equal parts of both. The driver shifted from low to high by using foot pedals. Gasoline was fed by gravity into the carburetor from a tank located in the rear, and if a hill being climbed was long and steep, the engine sputtered and died for want of fuel. The solution was to back up the hill.

Uncle Tom and Laney's mailbox was located next to ours near our front gate. From there, the road ran down a steep hill. Near the bottom, the driver had to negotiate a sharp left turn into Laney's lane. Sometimes, Uncle Tom, after loafing at Wayne's store, approached the mailbox and the lane too fast and he would haul back on the steering wheel yelling "Whoa! Whoa!" forgetting for the moment that he did not have a team of horses hitched to the front of his Model T.

Henry Sunderman (called "Andah" because when he spoke, he strung his phrases together with the word andah) had a 1932 Plymouth. Unlike the model T, it had a clutch, but therein lay the difficulty. Andah had the habit of pressing the accelerator to the floorboard and releasing the clutch. The car jumped about three feet and the engine died. Also, he sometimes got going so fast (about forty) he couldn't steer the automobile. On one occasion, he sideswiped a concrete bridge between Duff and his home. Thinking there was something wrong with his car, Andah consulted the blacksmith, Ed Ermert. "Ed," he said, "There is something wrong with the Plymouth. When I start her up, andah let the clutch out, she jumps up in the air andah the engine dies, andah when I do get goin' andah I'm goin' along there, she goes too fast." Ed knew what the problem was—he had sat on the store porch and watched Andah take off. So Ed said, "Andah, I'll see what I can do." He placed a wooden block under the accelerator so it could be depressed only so far. Thereafter, Andah had much smoother starts and he putted merrily on his way at a maximum speed of twenty miles per hour.

Henry (Andah) Sunderman.

Andah parked his Plymouth in a drive-through granary—one of those structures with doors on both ends, so that one could drive the team and wagon in, unload the grain, and then pull out the other side. It had been constructed on a mound so that rainwater would not collect under the granary and cause stored grain to draw moisture. The mound caused Andah a lot of difficulty because he had to come to a stop on top of the mound, and, failing that, would simply roll out the other side. One day, he was having a particularly difficult time. He had pulled into the granary three times, only to roll right on out the other side. Finally, on his fourth pass, someone yelled "Close the doors," and before Andah could roll on through, the doors were closed, the Plymouth banged into them and came to a stop.

Johnny Fenneman was another Model T driver. Johnny came around the corner of Wayne Hall's store too fast to make the turn, and drove into the deep ditch across the road. The porch boys and some of the men lifted his car out of the ditch. While Johnny was inside the store trading, the porch boys went into action. We lifted a rear wheel off the ground and placed a stick of wood under the axle very close to the wheel (so it couldn't be seen) and scraped a few rocks around the tire so that it appeared that the tire was resting on the surface of the roadway, when in fact it was suspended a half inch or so. Johnny got in his flivver, waved goodbye smiling his crooked, goofy smile, revved up the gas and magneto, let out the clutch, and nothing happened—he just sat there, looking foolish.

He looked over at us, favored us with another smile, and said, "I'll try her again." He tried a few more times, with the same result. Then he got out, looked under the hood and under the car, and couldn't find anything wrong and didn't spot the chunk of stove wood, so he scratched his head, and repeated the process. Same result. Meanwhile, young boys on the store porch shouted advice and encouragement to Johnny, stifling their glee in having pulled such a great joke on him. Finally, he discovered the cause of his difficulty and we shoved his car off the piece of stove wood. Another favorite trick was to place watermelon rinds under the tires so that the car would sit there, its wheels spinning until the tires wore through the rind.

Alex Lemond, story teller, never did learn to drive. He even took driving lessons determined to master the operation of the infernal machine, but it was a frustrating and humiliating struggle. He couldn't seem to get the timing right in steering the automobile, and had great difficulty going around corners. Invariably, as he approached a corner and was required to turn, he cranked the steering wheel too soon and drove into the ditch. Naturally, his failed attempts were a topic of conversation on the store porch, and every Valentine's Day, Alex received a couple of irritating reminders of his failure.

BE MY VALENTINE

Every Valentine's Day I am prompted to recall another great institution in Duff—the sending of Valentines. Not the kind with hearts and flowers and mushy verses. These Valentines were ugly, printed on cheap paper, cost a penny, and included a cartoon character and a verse. The cartoon character, always extremely ugly, was engaged in doing the thing described in the verse. Usually, the valentine exaggerated some perceived character flaw of the recipient. If a man drank too much, the cartoon depicted a man turning into a snake which was emerging from a whiskey bottle, and the doggerel read:

A man transformed to a reptile!
A direful change that would be.
But in you the Booze demon is working
A change as dreadful to see.

Dad was sure to get one of those, and it made him mad as hell—he was extremely sensitive and in denial about his drinking. Mom always received one which compared her with the "Old Woman Who Lived in a Shoe, Who Had So Many Children, She Didn't Know What to Do." She just laughed,and threw it in the stove.

Another depicted a lady who tended to "doll up," like Annie Stapleton. The verse was entitled "Mrs. Overdress," and said:

Your poor husband slaves all day
To dress you in this silly way
But worse and worse, each year, you get
While he gets deeper into debt.

RADIO BUG

YOU LISTEN MORNING, NOON AND NIGHT
TO TALES OF GORE AND HOOEY!
THE NEIGHBORS HOPE YOU DIE OF FRIGHT
BEFORE THEY ALL GO SCREWY!

MADE IN U.S.A.

Annie didn't care—she, along with Nellie Sunderman and Ruth Jones sent most of the valentines, so she knew it was sent by one of her friends.

A man who was perceived to be hen-pecked, like Stanley Peach, was depicted wearing a bridle and being driven by his wife:

To bridle and bit you meekly submit
Like a horse that's been trained to obey
A horse? No an ass would be more in your class,
Such a lack of all spunk you display.

Stanley was a small man and his wife Gladys was a spitfire. I had believed the story that she had broken a set of dishes, throwing them one at a time at Stanley, but when I asked her if the story was true, she denied it, saying she had thrown only a few cups and saucers at him. Furthermore, she said, "Stanley and I fought but he held his own—it was pretty much knock-down-and- drag-out."

Frank Heowener (Buck's dad), who never owned a car and drove a team of horses around town received this one:

You dirty, cruel savage, you haven't as much wit
In your ugly, stupid head, as the seat on which you sit.
From that frightful-looking mug of yours, as from a water spout
A steady stream of curses is always flowing out
And the horses who have got such a brute as you for master,
May rightfully consider that life is but disaster.

Mae Osborn always received one entitled "Miss Gossip":

Because you put folks "in a hole"
With talk that's vile and cheap
I'd like to see you in a hole—
A BIG one—six feet deep!

Hugo Lemond received several with the theme of "Tightwad;"

They say one day you spent a cent
But I, for one must doubt it
You never, never could survive
A single day without it

All the old drivers, Alex Lemond, "Andah" Sunderman, and Tom Songer received ugly missives entitled, "Reckless Driver;"

You drive like you are either
Stinkin' drunk or fast asleep
Some day you're gonna end up
In a big ditch—six feet deep!

Sometimes, the valentines contained some truth as applied to the receiver, but not always. Each storekeeper was sure to get one which showed him with his thumb on the scales when weighing merchandise even though he was honest. Even the school teachers, highly respected and without a hint of scandal, would read:

You think you know all the answers
You know what it's all about
Why don't you get an eraser
And just go rub yourself out?

When the valentine hit close to the bone, or if the receiver was particularly sensitive, such as Hugo E. Songer, he would get mad as hell. I made sure I went to the stores after the mail arrived on Valentines Day. Monzola Maxey, would come storming in, waving her crutch and the ugly Valentine in the air, her gray-green eyes blazing, accusing everyone in sight of doing the dirty, dastardly deed of sending that "damned old ugly Valentine. And when I find out for sure who it was, there is going to be hell to pay." Monzola had a withered right leg, the result of infantile paralysis, but by God, she was a Maxey and nobody was going to insult her and get away with it! Accusations flew, denials were made, followed by a new round of rumors that someone had admitted sending the offending verse, leading to new threats of revenge. It always took a couple of weeks for the townspeople to settle down after Valentine's Day.

THE CHARACTERS

Duff's townspeople were just themselves, rarely pretending to be anyone or anything they were not. If you asked to take their picture, they would oblige and stand there, unsmiling, staring into the eye of the camera. The proof is in the photographs. It was in the days before advertising was pervasive, before television, and Madison Avenue's attempt to make everyone the same. (You and 100 million other beer drinkers are told you can show your individuality by drinking a Bud.) Many had their own "bywords" which they seemed to have developed to fit their personalities. They never seemed contrived or "made up." Wayne Hall said "doggone;" Ed Ermert, "by-jacks;" Jim Songer, "by-gad;" Elmer Small, "dog-sarn;" and if you met Alex Lemond on the road and said, "It sure is a pretty day Alex," he was likely to sigh, "Yes, it's a beautiful day overhead—not many going that way," and Willis Stilwell often said: "Just so I get to heaven by the skin of my teeth." Bill Sunderman said, "Well, I don't know, maybe," and when you saw Bill coming down the road, you could see his lips moving as he started talking to you long before you were within earshot. Luther Bailey's by-word was: "A shaw." Once Marvin Stapleton, Babs Small, and Leon Songer filched some small cigars from Charlie Spurlock's store and crawled under the Christian church to smoke them. Luther, who lived across the road from the church, saw the boys puffing away under there and scurried to Nellie Sunderman's to report, "A shaw Nell, them boys are gonna set the church house on fire."

Leonard Weisheit, a big clumsy guy who wore a soft cap and bib overalls, said "By-God," with a strong nod of the head for emphasis, finishing his sentences with the word "along." Supposedly, Leonard first used this unusual speech mannerism when his Model T was rolled into a pile of scrap iron by a freight train at the crossing east of

Duff and pushed down the track for some distance. Crawling from the wreckage with only cuts and bruises, he said, "By God Fellers, that was a hell of a jolt along."

Leonard smoked a large curved pipe that nearly rested on his chest, and it seemed like he spent half his time messing with that pipe. One afternoon at Wayne's store, Leonard had just finished stuffing it full of tobacco and put it down to reach for an Orange Crush in the icebox. While his attention was diverted, someone poked a .22 shell with the bullet removed, into the bowl of his pipe. Opening his softdrink, Leonard sat down contentedly to enjoy his softdrink and a smoke. He fired her up and shortly thereafter, an explosion blew the bowl of the pipe apart. Leonard said, "By God, fellers, a joke's a joke but that's agoin' too fer along." Leonard wasn't very smart and perhaps he knew it, so he made up for it by speaking profoundly. Even if the topic was the weather, Leonard responded as if he were speaking from Mt. Olympus. He was very stubborn—once he made up his mind about something, you couldn't change it with a team of wild horses.

In late middle age, Leonard married Myrtle Barnett. Everyone thought it was a marriage made in heaven—otherwise, neither would have found anyone to marry in Duff. After they were married a few weeks, Leonard and Stanley Peach were walking the railroad track to the clay mine, when Stanley related to him in worried tones, "Leonard, I surely do hate to be the one to tell you this, but I think Ed Ermert is trying to get next to Myrtle. Why, just the other day, I saw him with his arm around her. Leonard, you better keep your eye on Ed." Leonard, startled at this news, turned on his heel, and without a word, started back to Duff. Stanley, suddenly anxious about Leonard's reaction called out to him, "Where you goin', Leonard?" and without breaking his stride, Leonard yelled back over his shoulder, "I'm going to kill the son-of-a-bitch." Stan ran after him, apologizing and pleading with him to stop but had a difficult time convincing him he had made it up. Only Leonard would believe that Ed Ermert and Myrtle had gotten together!

Otto Weisheit, butcher, and his son Leonard.

Leonard and Myrtle Weisheit, on their wedding day.

All newly married couples got a shivaree (charivari). It was supposed to be a surprise, but the couple knew it was in the offing, so they could have a supply of soft drinks and cake on hand. The entire town turned out. People drummed a tattoo on the side of the house with sticks, beat on dishpans or shook a tin can with rocks in it, and fired shotguns in the air. When Kathleen Peach and Earl Tabor were shivareed, her father, Lee Peach, a clay miner with access to dynamite, hung sticks of dynamite from tree limbs and set them off. It was customary for the couple to allow the noise-making to go on for a while, after which they would emerge from the house and be showered with rice, wheat, etc., and then they would treat the crowd to soft drinks and cake. In Leonard and Myrtle's case, after an extended period of shivareeing, it became clear they weren't coming out. Quick as the bang of a dishpan, someone was on top of the house placing a tub over the chimney. Soon, Leonard emerged from the front door, choking and gasping, pulling on his long johns as he came. Since Leonard had not played by the rules, the consequences got worse. Someone obtained a wheel barrow, filled it with water, and Leonard was ridden up and down the road. Soon tiring of that, they rode him on a rail. Waterlogged and exhausted, Leonard allowed as to how, "By God, fellers, that's agoin' too fer along." And indeed it was.

August Feller was a miser. We didn't know much about his early life, except that he had worked on the railroad on a section crew, had been married once, and had lost money in the failure of a Huntingburg bank in 1930. As a result, he didn't trust banks and it was common knowledge that he kept a substantial amount of cash in his home. He had been robbed at gun-point twice and almost killed the second time when he was lured to the railroad yards in Huntingburg for the supposed purpose of reuniting with his ex-wife.

Money was a sickness with August. Everyone was poor, but he chose to live in extreme poverty and go about in rags. Living alone in a shack on an isolated road near the Kessner covered bridge, he walked everywhere he went. He scarcely ever talked, although he would linger at the stores when he came to buy food, presumably in

August Feller, Miser

need of some human companionship. One day he and I were sitting on a lumber pile watching a croquet game in back of Spurlock's store, and I was startled when he scooted over and asked me what I wanted to do in life. I told him I didn't know. He said, "I have one bit of advice for you, Charlie, and that is to save your money."

During the early 1940s, August moved to Duff into the house in which Leonard and Myrtle had started their marriage. He had become too frail to walk the two miles from his place near the confluence of Elk Creek and Patoka river. He spent more time in the stores now, but the boys were a little apprehensive in approaching August. It was rumored he carried a gun. On winter days we often pitched pennies at cracks in the floor (closest winning the pennies thrown), and someone would drop a penny near August. Everyone would deny having dropped it and finally, when August was asked, he would "admit" that he had, and get down on all fours looking for it.

One cold winter when August still lived on the farm, someone said, so that August could overhear, that Clyde Voelkel's river bottom which was near August's place, was frozen over and Clyde had placed an ad in the *Jasper Herald* announcing that his bottom land was available for ice skating at fifteen cents per person. August scurried out, saying they could skate on his bottom land for ten cents.

In the fall of 1950 August's health began to fail in a serious way. He had a large untreated rupture and was generally debilitated. He called to me one day as I walked down the alley and asked if I would split some wood. I did, carried it in, and he asked me to split some more.

That was the first time I had even been in August's house. It was dark, dingy, and dirty. His table was covered with tin cans with the lids bent back—some empty and others half full of uneaten food. A small wood stove sat in the center of the room and August lay on a bench which served as a bed near the stove. "When I am out of wood," he said, "I pour kerosene on the floor and light it and it warms me up." "August," I said, "that is very dangerous! You could burn your house down."

He showed me a large abdominal rupture and said it had been

giving him some trouble. One evening, Dan Martin, who lived across the street and down the hill, happened to look out his window and saw that August's house was on fire. He ran to the Jones' who lived next to August, crying and screaming that August was burning up. Soon, other folks appeared on the scene, including Paulie Davis, who climbed on top of the Jones house and saved it by dousing it with buckets of water that were handed up to him. But it was too late to help August. Harold Hilgeman and I were returning from a movie in Huntingburg when we saw a large red glow in the sky over Duff. After the fire cooled, his torso was found, as well as a metal box containing the charred remains of several thousand dollars. Poor August!

WHEAT THRESHING

As soon as I was old enough to stop hiding behind my mother's skirt when the threshing machine engine came hissing, huffing, and puffing up the road to our driveway, I began working at wheat threshing—the most enjoyable event of the summer. Gillie Sunderman's threshing rig consisted of a steam engine and a separator. The separator, pulled from farm to farm by the steam engine, separated wheat, oat and barley grain from the straw and chaff.

The separator required level ground and many barnlots were not level, so holes were dug on the uphill side to accommodate its wheels. Gillie Sunderman was a regular whirling dervish when he was setting up his machine. Once the separator was in place, the steam engine backed off and a long belt ran from a pulley on the engine to a pulley on the separator to provide the necessary power. Local farmers divided into "companies" of eight or ten members, each farmer providing a team and wagon and two workers, including himself. Some drove the team and wagon which shuttled from field to barn lot, others "pitched" wheat bundles onto the wagons, and still others carried the newly threshed wheat to the granary. My first job was carrying water to the wheat pitchers in the field and to anyone else on the threshing crew who needed a cold drink of water on a hot July day. As soon as the machine was set up and ready to go, I would find a jug, fill it with fresh water, and hitch a ride on one of the wagons to the field. In most instances, the farmer paid me fifty cents for the day.

As I got a little older, various farmers hired me as a pitcher, or as a carrier. I much preferred carrying because that was where the action was. It was near the steam engine and separator. The whir of belts, pulleys, conveyors, and sprocket wheels on the separator, and the chugging of the steam engine, especially when its "governor" opened as it came under a load, made the area noisy. Dust and chaff filled the air.

It was organized confusion with a lot of action. Teamsters turned the air blue yelling and swearing at their sometimes terrified teams as they pulled loaded wagons alongside the separator; while at the same time, empty wagons rattled out to the fields for another load. Gillie Sunderman moved at a half run all day long, oiling the moving parts to keep the rig operating smoothly, and there was constant joking around among the carriers. Some wheat always spilled around the spout from which the golden grain flowed, and the farmer would shovel it up at the end of the day. But when wheat was spilled by a careless carrier at the Tony Hopf farm, Tony saw it and began cussing out the carrier in German, telling him in clear terms that he didn't want to see any more wheat spilled that day.

The by-product of the threshing process was a huge mountain of straw. The farmer usually built his own straw stack because he knew how he wanted it done. Ideally, the stack should have a conical shape so that when the straw "settled," the stack would shed water. All over the countryside a strawstack, almost as large as the barn, was as much a part of the rural landscape as the barn itself.

Once, in desperation, a farmer asked me to build his stack. I knew it was a hot, dirty job, but I was proud of having been asked, so I took a pitchfork and climbed onto the pile of straw that the blower was beginning to make. The task was to fork the straw toward the edges of the pile, leaving a depressed area in the middle, which the blower operator continuously filled. First one had to judge the size of the farmer's crop in order to decide the size of the stack. Threshing of wheat and oats was always done in July, and the day was hot and dry because you could not thresh in damp weather.

Imagine yourself in a gale force wind full of straw and chaff. The blower had a hood on it with moveable parts that allowed the blower operator to direct the flow of straw both left and right and up and down. Sometimes, out of pure cussedness, he would direct the flow at the stack builder and sometimes it was inadvertent. Either way, he acted like it was accidental, and the eyes and ears and clothing of the stack builder soon filled with straw and chaff. Unfortunately, I must have done the job well enough because I found myself building the stack at every farm. The truth is, it was a job that no one wanted to do, and the farmer would rather pay someone else than build it himself.

Gobby Collins described an incident involving Leonard Weisheit when threshing was taking place at Hugo Lemond's farm.

Leonard was building the stack and young Cletus Gambill was sitting on top of the separator with a set of ropes in each hand manipulating the spout at the end of the long pipe through which the straw was blasted from the machine. Clete was a reasonable fellow, but occasionally the temptation became too strong, with Len's broad back right there in front of him, and oh so inviting. He "accidentally" aimed the blast of straw at poor old Len, who was smothered in straw and suddenly appeared out of the maelstrom shaking his fist and waving his pitchfork in a threatening manner, at Clete. Clete made out with signs that he didn't do it on purpose and old forgiving Len trustingly went on with his work until Clete gave in once again to the awful temptation that overwhelmed him! He laid the straw on Len again and Len, saying "that's agoin' too fer along and I've had about enough of that foolishness," slid off the straw pile and announced that he was quitting.

Alarmed, Clete waved for the machine to be shut down and caught Len as he was stubbornly making his way toward his Model T. Clete knew that if Len quit, he, being next youngest with the threshing crew, would automatically be forced into Len's vacated job. He didn't want that! Clete followed Len toward his car pleading and begging that if Len would come back, he promised to be extra careful to not hit him with even a handful of straw. He even got Len a glass of lemonade, which cooled Len down quicker that anything. Len liked to be coaxed and with much coaxing and promises of extra good treatment, Len was persuaded to resume his straw stack making. "Now looka here," Len shook his stubby finger in Clete's face, "if I git hit with that straw again, I'm comin' off that there pile and I'm comin' after you with this here pitchfork." Gillie gave Clete a hard look and opined, "If I wanted to be sure of my job, I would be sure that this here machine ain't gonna be shut down anymore this day!" Clete climbed back on the machine and signaled for the startup.

About an hour after all this happened and the operation was proceeding smoothly and old Hugo Lemond was grinning broadly from his vantage point under the big maple tree, fate took a hand once again. It had been so peaceful, the constant roar of the threshing machine, the puffing of the steam engine, wagons shuttling from field to barnlot, and bushels and bushels of golden wheat finding their way into Hugo's granary. But suddenly a crack appeared in that peaceful scene.

It all started when Hugo noticed old Len stiffen and grab his backsides. Len looked all around and with a shrug, wiped the sweat from his face with a big red handkerchief and turned back to his work. The machine roared on and Clete carefully kept the spewing straw on the opposite side of the stack from Len. Hugo kept his eye on Clete and Len because of the earlier fracas and because he didn't want that flow of money to stop going to his granary. Then he saw Len grab his backside again and wondered what was causing this peculiar activity! Len staggered around there on the straw stack and glared all around, glancing up at Clete and once again went back at his stacking. Hugo relaxed once more, but kept a sharp eye on Len there on the stack. Suddenly, Len grabbed frantically at his rear with both hands and dropping his pitchfork, jumped sprawlingly to the ground. Hugo ran over to him along with the threshing boss, Gillie Sunderman and yelled, "Now what's the matter Len?" "There now, by God," Len squalled, "thar's bees in that stack, and I done been stung for the third time, and I ain't gonna stay up there and get stung ever few minutes!" "Why whoever heard of such," exclaimed Hugo, who was by this time alarmed and agitated, "bees don't nest in wheat!" "Well, all I know is that I done been stung three times, which is agoin' too fer along, and I ain't goin' up there again," Len stated flatly, with a real stubborn, determined look on his face. Gillie turned and waved the shut down sign to Bill Fark, the engine man. Blowing the steam whistle to signal the shut down, Bill pulled the hook. The roar of the machine died down and it was suddenly quiet. The smooth operation of a few minutes ago had ceased.

Old Hugo felt the pull on his bank account and with red face, turned furiously on Clete perched above on the threshing machine. "Clete, says he, "what the dang nang are ye' doin' up there?" Clete threw up his hands in innocence, "Hugo, I ain't doin' nothin' but blowing this here straw and none of that on Len," he exclaimed! "Well," screamed the pocketbook-wounded Hugo, "who the dang nang is doin' what to Len here then? I can't stand for all this nonsense!" Turning to Gillie, he said, "Just what are ye' gonna do about this situation?" Gillie thought about it for a moment and upon questioning Len, determined that it wasn't all Len's imagination, so he climbed up on the straw stack to check it out for bees. Crawling around on the stack, Gillie yelled, "Why there ain't no bees up here, Len." A moment later, he yelled loudly and clapped his hand to his backside, looking around wildly. "I told yuh," Len laughed, slapping his leg with his old straw hat. Gillie came sliding off the stack with a grim look on his face. He opened his clenched fist and said, "Looka here what I've got!" Laying in his hand was an air rifle pellet. "When it hit me I clapped my hand back there and that pellet was a hangin' in that patch on my pocket," Gillie breathed excitedly. "Now we gotta find out where they are a-comin' from and get that son-of-a-gun! Spread out men," yelled Gillie, "look up in th' trees and in th' barn and all around—when we catch 'em ther really gonna get it!" Not more than a couple of winks later, he motioned them over under a gnarled old sycamore by the barn. Looking up in the tree, he said calmly, "Do you fellers see what I see?" They all looked up in the sycamore and saw young Lee Lemond shooting at some sparrows with an air rifle! The group of men standing under the sycamore staring up at young Lee perched on a limb, and grinning like a jackass, were not to be trifled with! Gillie demanded, "Lee, get down out of that tree right now." Lee, looking down at the unsmiling faces below, responded "I'm not sure I'm safe if I come down there!" Gillie said, "Either you come down or we're comin' up there after you, and if we have to do that we will kick your ass all the way back to Duff!" And then he added, "If I wasn't a friend of your Dad, I would do it anyway! And if I catch you shootin' around here agin, I'll break that blasted BB gun in a thousand pieces." Lee considered the matter and, grinning broadly, slid down the tree and started backing away from the threshers, stating defensively that he was only shooting sparrows and that he couldn't help it if Len got in the way. Some of the men started after him and Lee wisely got into high gear and headed for Duff on the double. The threshing machine was started up again and the wagons began to unload again and wheat began to flow out of the threshing spout into the burlap sacks that men bore to Hugo's granary. Hugo again perched contentedly on an upturned bucket in the shade and smiled broadly as the dollars rolled into his bank account. Life does have its little moments, Hugo must have thought, but the end result is what really matters. He looked contentedly at his broad farmstead, appreciating the bounty which was his to enjoy. His happiness broadened as the afternoon wore away and he dozed in the shade of the old sycamore.

With Len it was not so. He sweated through another hot, sultry day, as he had all the days of his life. His earnings would never accumulate to bring him comfort and an easy life. He would have to work hard, at jobs that others declined, all of his life to make ends meet. Len wasn't complaining. He had the necessities of life and was a healthy, strong man. His house wasn't more than a shack and his car was old and battered. But he had friends aplenty and that was very important to Len. "So let the days roll by," said Len, "we'll all come to the same end—we cain't take anything with us anyway."

Gilbert Sunderman's threshing rig on the move. Hugo E. Songer astride the water tank; Gillie Sunderman on the ground.

THE STORY TELLERS

Television was unheard of and the adults had even grown up without radio. They had learned to entertain themselves. Some of them, such as Louis Mayo and Alex Lemond, had a natural gift for story telling. Alex grew up in neighboring Velpen, Duff's arch rival in baseball. When Alex was a young boy, he got a little red lantern for Christmas. He and a friend got the idea of making a big kite to tie the lantern onto so they could fly it over Velpen. It was the turn of the century before anything shone in the night sky besides the moon and stars. Alex and his friend took their kite out on the hill south of Velpen on a windy night and, hooking the lantern onto the kite's tail, watched it lift off in a big puff of wind.

The little red lantern was swinging back forth, high over Velpen. It was fun, lying there on the hillside, enjoying the ballet of the little red lantern! Tiring finally, they pulled the kite down and went home to bed. The next day, at Lemond's store, people were all abuzz about the strange light in the sky the night before. It was seen as a bad omen of unhappy things to come for the citizens of Velpen, or even perhaps for the state, or God forbid, the country. Old men sat in the spring sun warming themselves on the store porch, speculating about the cause of this strange phenomenon. Women clattered door-to-door, wondering whether past sins had brought them to some horrible fate. Headlines in the *Petersburg Press* were startling, "Strange Light In Sky Over Velpen," with a full column of scary comments portending some doom. While all of this went on, the little "men from Mars" huddled guiltily in their rooms. The kite and the little red lantern were hidden fast under a large brushpile, never to see the light of day again. Finally, when nothing traumatic came to pass in the village, and the light in the sky faded in the people's memories, little Alex and friend breathed a sigh of relief. Life resumed its jaded pace and the most exciting event of the day, once more was the arrival of the noon train, when it rolled into town, steaming and whistling, and then puffed importantly on its way to Princeton.

There was a "yaller" coon-hound in Velpen which belonged to no one except the entire town. He was of uncertain ancestry, although some said several dog generations earlier his ancestor had arrived there with an early settler from South Carolina: that he was a breed of southern hound dog that had originally crossed the Bering straits thousands of years before.

The townspeople called him Tramp. Tramp whiled away the day on Lemond's store porch listening no doubt to the discussions and local gossip, and, being "at large," was totally dependent upon the kindness of townspeople and strangers for a living.

Sometimes, unlike the townspeople, Tramp became bored with the goings on at the store porch and wandered down to the depot when he heard Old #23 whistle for the Velpen crossing.

As the train pulled out, Tramp would jump on the rear platform of the last car and ride the eleven miles to Huntingburg. For some reason, he by-passed Duff, which lay between the other two towns. Whether he had a lady friend in Huntingburg or craved the anonymity, no one ever knew. After a week or two on the town, he would catch the noon train back to Velpen and resume his rightful place among the other loafers on Lemond's store porch.

Duff's greatest story teller was Uncle Louis Mayo. (Anyone over seventy years of age was called "Aunt" or "Uncle.") His stories were outrageous lies, but he got sore if you expressed doubt or laughed at them. By far, the most entertaining aspect was the way he told them. At critical points in the story, he clucked, cooed, and rubbed his forehead, as if to say "this is almost unbelievable, but it's true." One bitter cold winter day, he had looked at the usual "signs" and could tell that the temperature was going to fall even further overnight. He had walked back to his pond and noticed that it was covered with ducks. "I'm gonna get me some of them ducks when their feet become frozen in the ice," he said to himself. "Sure 'nuf, the next

Lloyd (Gobby) Collins and Alex Lemond, Story Tellers.

morning, I got up and rinsed my face, and when I threw out the water, it froze before it hit the ground. "Oh," he clucked and cooed, "I knew I was gonna get me some ducks. I walked back to the pond and just as I predicted, there they were, quacking and squawking, their feet frozen fast in the ice. As I approached, I decided to make the ducks raise a ruckus, so I threw my arms in the air and yelled 'Shoo,' and the ducks flew away with the pond."

"One day during a terrible thunderstorm, I made a dash for my barn, and as I reached there, I grabbed the iron handle of the barn door. At that instant, a terrific lightning bolt struck the barn, traveled down the metal of the door, into my arm, through my body and right leg, knocking the heel off my boot." Rubbing his forehead, clucking, cooing, and pausing for dramatic effect, he continued, "I was dazed for a moment, didn't quite know where I was, and then I looked up at the sky, shook my fist, and yelled, "Old man, if you're gonna get me, you're gonna hafta put in a little more powder."

One sultry summer day, the loafers on the store porch were complaining about the heat. Uncle Louis scoffed at the complaints, and allowed as how the summers were not near as hot as they used to be. At that point, you knew another story was coming. He cleared his throat, rubbed his forehead, clucked, and said, "About twenty years ago, I was shucking popcorn. Every once in a while, I would say, Giddyup to the mules and they would pull the wagon up a few more feet as we passed down the row. It got hotter and hotter until I thought I couldn't stand it no more. The temperature continued to climb when suddenly, the popcorn commenced to poppin' in the field. The mules thought it was snowin' and laid down and froze to death."

In summer, one topic of conversation was sure to be the animals and snakes we had seen. Someone related how he had been chased by a blue racer, which truly seemed to have the strange characteristic of following people who encountered it. Someone else told how a milk-snake had preceded him to the barn that evening and sucked the old cow dry. At one-upmanship, Uncle Louis was not to be outdone. He thought those snake stories mighty puny. "I was hoein' corn the other day and had stopped to sharpen my hoe with a whetstone I carried. As I stood there sharpenin' the hoe blade, I happened to look up the hill, and here came this hoop snake, his tail in his mouth, rollin' straight toward me." He paused, rubbed his forehead, and clucked, as his listeners waited to hear what happened next. "At the last second, I jumped aside, and stuck out my hoe handle. The hoop snake bit that hoe handle on the run, and then continued rollin' down the hill. Within a minute or two, that hoe handle was swelled up bigger than my knee."

Lewis Hochmeister, one of Duff's best hunters, said he had seen a wild turkey that morning while squirrel hunting. That was a rare sighting at that time, because wild turkeys had been killed off during the previous decades. But Uncle Louis "harrumped" and made it clear he didn't think much of that turkey story. "Several years ago, there was a gang of wild turkeys came through here that numbered about fifteen hundred and they were led by a peacock. There was about a thousand men chasin' them and it happened that only four turkeys were killed and me and my brother John killed them." Then, as if that story was insufficient to overcome Lewis' story of having seen a single turkey, Uncle Louis continued: "I had gone turkey hunting several years ago and hadn't killed a single bird. As I was nearing home, I spotted twelve turkeys roostin' in a row on a single limb. I had only one load left and I'd shore like to get more than one turkey. So I raised up my old muzzle-loader, took careful aim, shot and split the limb the turkeys were roostin' on, caught their toes in that crack, and got 'em all with one shot." It was impossible to outdo Uncle Louis Mayo when it came to story telling.

Lem Small, no slouch at story telling himself, tried to top Uncle Louis one day when he said: "Uncle Louis, my grandpa Peter Small told me that when he first came to this part of the country, the trees were so big you couldn't hardly get around 'em in the woods. He said that you and him met each other when you were both pullin' loads of hay through the woods and the path was too narrow to allow the carts to pass. He said he backed his load onto the limb of one of those big trees and let you go by." Uncle Louis looked at Lem for a moment, scowled, rubbed his forehead, clucked, and said, "Son, I think your grandpa lied."

Louis Mayo, Story Teller extraordinaire.

JONATHAN WALKER

One winter evening, a number of old loafers were at Spurlock's store, and we had all settled down for some serious talk, when the old men began talking about pioneer times. Charlie Spurlock explained that the Paynes and Spurlocks were neighbors in Kentucky and both families decided to move to Indiana and enter land. The year was 1818. Indiana had just become a state. William Spurlock couldn't leave because his wife Patsy was pregnant, so James Payne came on ahead. They agreed to connect up later.

When Patsy Spurlock and her baby were able to travel, the family crossed the Ohio River at the falls near Louisville and began the trip along the Buffalo Trace through Southern Indiana. William had packed two horses for the trip—one was loaded with their belongings, rifle, ax, skillets, and quilts. Patsy and the newborn rode the other horse, son James behind his mother. The oldest child, Manerva Jane, and her father walked all the way.

James Payne had written and told them to leave the Buffalo Trace where it intersected the Yellow Banks Trace (which came up from Rockport, and was called Yellow Banks by the Indians) as they approached the Mudholes (south of Portersville) and then head south, reaching the Patoka River at the site of a mill (now Jasper) and then head west. When the road traversed a place called the Devil's Backbone, they would again be near the Patoka River where there was a ford (later, Kessners Bridge). James Payne had entered land on the south side of the river and the Spurlock entry was to be there as well. (This area, north of Duff near the Patoka River, came to be known as Crackersneck. The river doubled back, creating a narrow "neck" and most of the settlers were from the south, hence the name.) When they arrived at the river, they hallooed for James Payne, whose land bordered it. Payne helped them across the Patoka and they were all very excited about seeing the Paynes again and arriving at their new home.

Alex Lemond said that his ancestors had come from North Carolina, and one of them, a great-grandfather, was an Indian fighter and fist-fighter known all over the southern part of Indiana. His name was Jonathan Walker, and Alex didn't know much more about him. Later that evening, I asked Dad if he had ever heard of Jonathan Walker. Without hesitation he stated: "He was the greatest fighter around these parts in pioneer times." "Dad," I complained, "Why didn't you ever tell me about him before?" "You never asked," he said, "and besides, he's been dead a long time. He died even before my dad was born." Many years passed before I would learn more about Walker and what I found was fascinating. He was a Scot, born in North Carolina in 1790, and migrated with his brother Isaac, through Kentucky to Indiana Territory in about 1807. In 1811, he married Mary (Polly) Brenton, daughter of James and sister of Peter, founder of Petersburg, county seat of Pike County.

Walker reportedly fought Indians before moving to Indiana, and in the first year of his marriage, had a chance to call upon his experience. The Indians were still active on the frontier and there were frequent uprisings against the encroaching whites, as in 1807 when several settlers were killed. In 1811, Jonathan accompanied several hundred other men, including Peter and Henry Brenton, Woolsey Pride (who had built a fort at White Oak Springs near Petersburg) and Jonathan's friend, Purty Old Tom Montgomery, of what became Gibson County, to Tippecanoe with William Henry Harrison, governor of the Indiana Territory. On November 11th, they defeated the Indians, led by the Prophet, brother of the great Indian leader, Tecumseh, who was absent at the time of the battle. Purty Old Tom Montgomery shot and killed White Loon, one of the Indian leaders. In 1814, Jonathan was the first to enter land in Madison Township, across the Patoka River and north of where Duff was to be located, which began the so-called Irish Settlement. Soon, others of Scots-Irish descent followed and Madison and neighboring

Boone townships were settled by the Scots, a robust, well-educated, even sophisticated group of people, mostly Presbyterian. Many of their ancestors were lowland Scots who fled Scotland for northern Ireland because of persecution by English kings.

Jonathan liked to drink and he liked to fight, and soon gained a reputation for both along the Buffalo Trace. This thirty-foot wide Buffalo path ran from the salt licks of Kentucky to the falls of the Ohio river near Louisville and then for one hundred-twenty miles across southern Indiana to the Wabash river at Vincennes and across the river to the vast prairie lands of Illinois. Buffalo migrated for thousands of years along the Trace, the last small herd having been seen there in 1803, and it became a heavily traveled road used by pioneers to traverse thickly wooded Southern Indiana. Indiana had hardwood forests as far as the eye could see—there was an occasional clearing but you could travel all day and never get out of the deep woods until you reached a river.

At public gatherings, on holidays, and particularly on election day, Jonathan, a strapping, bare-knuckle brawler, would be there, stripped to the waist, challenging anyone to a fight. Jonathan was tall, narrow waisted, broad shouldered, and proud of his physique. Many men, even other fighters, feared him, not so much because they didn't like to fight, but for the brutal ending if they fought to win. If Walker thought the other man gave up, not because he was beaten, but because he hated a brutal fight, Walker would give him no peace until they fought to the finish. Sometimes Walker himself was dripping with blood when the fight was over.

Walker was not a bully or an aberration on the frontier. Fighting, as a recreational pursuit, was common. Some men even sharpened their thumb nails into a point for the sole purpose of gouging out the opponent's eye, and many a one-eyed man was found on the frontier. Walker once took a sled load of furs to Vincennes for trading purposes, and two men who thought they would have some fun at his expense, caused his horse to run away, scattering his furs. Walker found the men in a tavern, and beat the two of them senseless.

Walker never belonged to a church, but it seems he felt some guilt about his behavior. He wasn't concerned about the fighting; it was his occasional bouts of swearing that concerned him. One day Polly called to him that their sow was in their cornfield and Jonathan went after her. His dog caught and held the sow by the leg and Jonathan picked her up and threw her across his shoulder. The sow bit him on the backsides and Jonathan turned the air blue with profanity and threw the hog down with such force that she died. Jonathan was more concerned about the sin of swearing than the gash on his back or the loss of the sow. He moaned to his wife: "Polly, just think what that damned old hog caused me to do!"

Jonathan was at the county courthouse on a cold winter day, with snow and ice covering the ground, when he wagered that he could crawl on his hands and knees to the Patoka River, located a half mile south, swim the river and crawl back to the courthouse on his hands and knees. He won the bet. Jonathan was often present at the log courthouse at Portersville, the first county seat.

There was a deadening of trees near there. Litigants, after a full day's ride from around the county, prepared to spend the night, and built huge campfires from the dead trees. Whiskey sold for twenty-six cents a gallon and there was considerable merriment around the campfires. There were "fist and skull" fights and Jonathan and Absolom Harbison, a Revolutionary War soldier, were often the combatants. Apparently, things got out of hand on one occasion when Ab Harbison went after Jonathan with a knife. Ab was charged and tried for attempted murder, but found guilty of the lesser charge of battery. The two men must have fought often, because Harbison told the *Jasper Courier* that he was once compelled to wait four days to have his grist ground at the mill on the Patoka River at Jasper, and put in his time by fighting with Walker following a dispute over shooting at a mark, running a race with a big Indian, and "jumping for drinks" with the late Enoch Abel. In addition, he killed a bear in a tree which stood at what is now the corner of 7th and Jackson streets in Jasper.

In 1840, Jonathan and one Benjamin Taylor got into a dispute with a German shoemaker, Hudeman, in Huntingburg, near the site of the St. George Hotel. The altercation became physical and Hudeman was killed. Taylor left the area immediately and Jonathan was charged and tried for murder. He was defended by Judge Pitcher, a highly respected lawyer from Spencer County. (Abraham Lincoln often visited Judge Pitcher's office when he delivered pork and other produce for shipment to the Southland on the Ohio River, and in later years, when Lincoln visited Spencer County, he inquired of the location of Judge Pitcher's law office). The jury acquitted Jonathan, the evidence showing that Taylor had struck the fatal blow. Not long thereafter, Jonathan and Polly left the Irish settlement and entered land in the southeast corner of Dubois County near present day St. Henry. His homestead was near a pigeon roost, where millions of passenger pigeons, now extinct, roosted in the forest. They roosted in such great numbers that tree limbs broke under their weight, and only the strongest stubs of limbs remained in those forests. At twilight, heading for their roosts, they blackened the sky, their flocks measuring five miles wide and fifty miles or more in length. (The last passenger pigeon died in a Cincinnati zoo in 1914.)

Jonathan and Polly had ten children, five boys and five girls. Three of the sons, Sampson, Dessix, and Bloomfield, served in the Civil War. Bloomfield did not return. But what does all of this have to do with Duff? Jonathan and Polly died in the 1850s and Duff wasn't founded until 1882. However, Jonathan would have been acquainted with all his fellow Scots, particularly B.B.Edmonston, whom Dufftown was named after. In fact, Colonel Edmonston wrote of his friend Walker in 1879:

Among the early pioneers of this county was Jonathan Walker, who was large and powerfully built and probably the strongest man in this part of the state, judging from the number of fights he engaged in, and generally with the strongest men and almost always coming off victorious in a regular "fisticuff." Yet he was a good hearted man, always ready to share with those poorer than himself and ready to defend the weak from the assaults of the stronger. He never used anything but his fists in a fight. Oh, no! It was considered cowardly in those days to use a knife or other weapon.

There were many additional Duff connections, as we shall see, and Jonathan seems to have exerted a strong pull on his descendants. His grandson, Jonathan Walker, III, a Civil War veteran, got into an election day dispute with George and Joseph Corn over a horse race at Augusta in Pike County. Joe Corn struck Walker with brass knuckles, but Walker recovered, got Corn down, and was really laying it to him when George Corn, who was armed, came to the aid of his brother and shot Walker fatally through the body. Jonathan Walker III is buried between two other Civil War soldiers in the Miller cemetery just west of Duff. William Wayman, one of the soldiers and a traveling actor who decided to stay in this area, died at the home of my great grandfather, Floyd Songer.

Another grandson, Richard Walker, Bloomfield's son, after helping dig the grave for a child of John B. Lemonds at Payne cemetery, was headed home when his horse was frightened by the sudden appearance of a buggy. The horse ran away and threw Richard off, his head striking a tree. He was injured so seriously that he died within a few hours. The report of his death said:

He was a grandson of Jonathan Walker, one of the pioneers of this section, and like his ancestor, was rough and plucky to the end, swearing when he got up from the tree that if he got over the hurt, he'd "kill the damned horse."

The three Civil War sons married girls who lived in the vicinity of Duff, and Bloomfield's widow, Judah, lived in the August Feller house. Jonathan and Polly's oldest daughter Mary, called Betsy, married Richard Stilwell, also of the Duff community. Their son

Willis married Lizzie, my grandfather's sister, and they raised a large family on the place where I live now. Betsy and Richard's daughter, Elizabeth, married Peter Lemond, a Civil War soldier, and the couple lived in the house west of Spurlock's store. Peter Lemond had a hole in his right ear, put there by a minie ball at the Battle of Lookout Mountain. He also said of that battle that he was standing behind a good sized tree halfway up that mountain and something told him he had better move. A split second after he left the tree, a cannon ball reduced it to splinters. I remember Aunt Betty, as Elizabeth was called, and she is the source of much of the information about her grandfather, Jonathan Walker. Peter and Aunt Betty's oldest son was Alex, the storyteller. That brings us full circle from Jonathan to his connection with Duff.

It is the girls, the daughters of Peter and Aunt Betty Lemond, to whom I direct your attention. There was Maggie, married to Bill Soloman; Emma, married to Dan Gearner, and mother of Ben and Harold Gearner; Nancy, unmarried, who gave birth to Orville (Jum) and Virgil, and later married Andy Summers but had no children by him; Martha, who married Homer Osborn; and Lena (Laney), who married three times, and always kept a live-in after she was widowed from Adam Lotsegesell, the last of whom was Uncle Tom Songer. They were good-looking ladies: raucous, earthy, and sexually liberated. Some of them boarded the trains at crossings east of Duff and rode for a few miles with the train crew, just long enough, to the next stop.

Just after noon on a Monday, in 1897, Ed Stutsman was standing on the porch of the small post office building in Duff. He looked down the road and saw Bill Soloman, who had been working on the M.D. Lemond farm nearby, come up. Soloman confronted Stutsman, saying: "What the hell are you doing around my wife Maggie when I'm away?" Stutsman replied that he had not been at the Soloman house. Soloman called him a liar, and at the same time drew his revolver and fired two shots at Stutsman, the second of which found its mark, and Sutsman fell to the porch floor, mortally wounded. Soloman made no attempt to get away, was arrested, and tried for second degree murder. The townspeople's sympathy was with Soloman, and he was acquitted, the jury finding he was insane at the time of the act. It seems that Stutsman had persisted in his attention to Maggie, even after the two of them had been convicted of adultery in another county, and after he had been warned repeatedly to stay away from her. Soloman left a wife and two children.

Nancy and Martha were indicted for prostitution, the indictment oddly charging them with "unlawfully associating with women of bad character for chastity—on the public highways of said county, and in public church houses in Duff," that being the manner in which prostitution was charged at the time, even though their sexual liaison with men lay at the heart of the charge. Of course, women did not yet have the vote, so men could phrase the statutes anyway they wanted. A number of men, presumably the "johns," were called as witnesses for the state, and a number of Duff men and women, including my great-grandmother, Mary Ann Songer, were subpoenaed by the defense as character witnesses. The case never went to trial. Soon thereafter, Nancy sued Charlie Baker for bastardy, in what is today called a paternity suit. Before filing suit, apparently because she was unsure who the father was, she sent identical letters to Baker and Adorno Lindsey, alleging that each was the father of her child. Baker learned of the Lindsey letter, and when he went to court, his attorney subpoenaed Lindsey and his letter, and the judge threw out the case.

Dad told me that the father of Nancy's son, Jum, was a very smart man, a bridge builder. Jum was of high intellect, excelled in school, and won all the spelling contests. Rather than work at hard labor like most Duffers, Jum went to Wood's Switch, just east of Duff, on the Southern railroad, learned Morse code from L.C. Brown, and spent a career as a telegrapher for the railroad, and on seagoing ships during the war. In 1925 he built a crystal radio set, the first radio in Duff, at his grandmother Aunt Betty's house, and Duffers flocked there to hear the miracle of beautiful orchestra music, the first they had ever heard, coming in over the airwaves.

Martha sued Phineas Postlethwait for bastardy, but the child did not survive. She married Homer Osborn, one of the kindest, most gentle, Christian men I have ever known of whom I speak in another context. Homer was devoted to Martha. One person who knew them well said that Homer loved her precisely because of her raucous nature and dubious history—that it had the effect of balancing his goodness so that his own human nature was more even.

This person told me that in her wilder days, Martha was photographed in the nude from the backside, leaning over a counter, with her head turned to the right, a flower in her hair. The image was enlarged and featured in an area tavern. Homer learned of it and reputedly paid the tavern owner one hundred dollars for the picture. As a child, I spent some time visiting in their home and was most fascinated by their stereoscope, through which I viewed pictures in three dimensions of exotic places from around the world.

Emma's sons, Ben and Dan Gearner, carried on the tradition in the manner in which they conducted their lives. You will recall that Ben, the old veteran who had walked on the China Wall, was a regular on the store porch, and a hell-raiser. His brother Harold, the fiddler, was a professional hobo.

Laney (Lena), with whom Uncle Tom lived, was the one we spent the most time with. Her long dirt lane led west for nearly half a mile from the rock road in front of our house, ending at her hilltop home, which had a commanding view of Duff and surrounding farms. Laney was like Mother Nature herself, shown by her bounteous garden, and the row upon row of seed stock hanging from the rafters of her screened-in back porch which she had saved for next spring's garden. Many times, I sat in the shade of huge maple trees in Laney's front yard and enjoyed the view with her and Uncle Tom while listening to him play his fiddle. Laney, like her great-grandfather Jonathan Walker, was rough and plucky to the end.

THE CHURCHES

Duff had three church buildings, which from time to time, housed many denominations. The Church of Christ, sometimes called the Christian church, organized in 1868, and still meets today. There was also the Primitive Baptist Church, whose members were sometimes described as Hard-Shell Baptists. Its congregation was called "Little Flock." The church was founded in 1842 and first met at a log cabin in Dufftown until it built a church building in Duff, which doubled as a one room schoolhouse, just as it had in old Dufftown, until the new school was built across from the Songer homestead in 1914. The Little Flock Primitive Hard-Shell Baptist Church continued to meet in what had become over the years an old dilapidated building. Finally it bought the building built and occupied by the German Evangelical church organized in 1897 and disbanded in 1925.

The Church of Christ had a stable congregation which meets even today. Its members were the bedrock of the community—the ones who cautioned young children who were out too late in the evening that their mamas wanted them. They were staunch supporters of the school, and they were in the middle of community events—plays in the Odd Fellows Hall, quilting parties, and shivarees. In deference to the mischievous side of human nature, they also sent most of the ugly valentines, which was perhaps a not-so-gentle reminder to their neighbors to shape up!

They were, however, on good terms with the unchurched and the inebriates. Annie Stapleton, a stalwart member, would walk the half a block from her home to Wayne Hall's store. Customarily, Ben Gearner would be seated on the bench with his back to the wall. Annie would say with a big smile, her gold tooth shining, "Why Hi, Ben, how are you this morning?" and Ben would reply "I'm fine; how in the hell are you Annie?" and they would exchange a few pleasantries before Annie entered the store. Annie, a pretty lady with thick dark brown hair, dancing brown eyes and a great personality, called all the children "Hon," and if children were out and about on the streets too late in the evening, she was the one who would say, "You'd better run along home Hon, your momma wants you."

My Dad's parents, Jim and Louise, and his grandparents, Floyd and Mary Ann, had been Hard-Shell Baptists. Their practices had not changed during the century. (One of its sister churches was the Little Pigeon Primitive Baptist Church, in neighboring Spencer County, to which Thomas and Sarah Lincoln and son Abraham belonged.) The benches were hard and the sermons long, sometimes lasting two hours or more. There was a stoic, rugged pioneer spirit about their practices. Hardship was at the core of life and they conducted church services as if to say: "There should be nothing easy about this. Life is hard and so is making connection with the Almighty."

I was intrigued by their distinctive handshake which was a single, firm downward stroke, exchanged at the close of services. Central to their belief was humility in the face of God: that one is saved by the grace of God and not by good works. Furthermore, God had preordained events and every individual's fate was predestined as God guided him or her infallibly toward salvation. Their humility was demonstrated by the practice of foot-washing and while their stoicism might seem contradicted by a shedding of tears, emotion was shown quietly, and arose out of their humility and thankfulness in God's having "saved a wretch like me."

Long before "Amazing Grace" became a trendy song, it was the anthem of the Primitive Baptists. Tom France was the preacher for many years, and if you can see William Jennings Bryan in your mind's eye, you can visualize Tom France. He began his sermons quietly, gradually building to a thundering crescendo, tears streaming down his face. Pulling out a large white handkerchief, he loudly blew his nose, wiped his streaming tears, and then quietly began again. As I sat there squirming on the hard bench, I knew there was no hope that the sermon would end until this had happened seven or eight times, but the disappointment was almost overwhelming when I was certain this was the last crescendo, and he began again!

The Hard-Shell Baptists were strict about how the members conducted their lives, particularly with respect to drinking, and for a long time, Dad resisted joining. Finally, one emotion-filled day, he declared himself ready to accept Christ. In a few weeks, the congregation met on the banks of the Patoka river, a few yards upriver from the Kessner covered bridge, and as the members, standing on the riverbank in the shade of those great old sycamores that leaned out over the river, sang, "Shall we Gather at the River," Dad was baptized and his sins were washed away. For a while, fresh with the purity of the experience, Dad behaved, but he was a drinker, and the old devil alcohol beckoned him. He wasn't hypocritical about it—he started drinking again and stopped going to church.

Mom often accompanied Dad to Baptist services but was uncomfortable there. She continued her membership in the German Evangelical church in Huntingburg, which practiced sprinkling in the rite of baptism, while the Baptists had no stronger belief than baptism by immersion, preferably in a moving body of water, just as John the Baptist had baptized Jesus in the river Jordan. She always felt, perhaps with some justification, that the topic of the sermon on the Sundays she accompanied Dad was aimed at her: i.e., to be saved and enter the Kingdom of Heaven, you had to be immersed. Anything less condemned you to hell and damnation.

Years later, after the Baptists had stopped baptizing in the river and started using Norm and Mae Osborn's pond as their baptismal, I told Dad that it seemed there was an epidemic of sinning in Duff, particularly among the Baptists. He took me seriously and wondered why that was the case. "The reason seems to be," I said, "that Norm's pond is so full of washed-away sins, those being baptized actually absorb more sins than they had when they stepped in the water." "Aw, hell," was all he said.

For a number of years, before the Baptists took it over, the Holy Rollers occupied the German church building. The contrast couldn't have been greater between them and the Baptists! The latter approached God with fear and trembling, and when a member felt he had sinned in a significant way, he or she returned with great sorrow and humility, amid many quiet tears and loud nose-blowing. The Holy Rollers, on the other hand, were much more joyful, and there was playing of guitars, singing and testifying, and speaking in tongues. If a member sinned and stopped coming to church for a while, which was called backsliding, and then came back, there was great joy, and the member got special recognition. Laney Lotsgesell (Lena Lemond) backslid often, for the reason, I always thought, that it was great fun to come sliding back in. When Laney came back, there was an air of expectation in the room and when the service started, she took a throne-like chair on a riser at the front of the church. Then she began "testifying," telling in vivid detail how she had been tempted by the devil, had given in to the temptation, and then saw the error of her ways. Without pausing, the emotion of the moment led her into speaking in tongues; then the entire congregation began playing music, singing, circling Laney's chair, and testifying as one and all were swept into ecstasies of religious fervor. Near the conclusion of one such event, Laney stood, threw her arms in the air, and shouted: "I'm just gonna fly away to heaven," did a belly flop onto the floor and lay there waving her arms and legs, "flying" as it were.

Sis and I were seated in the back row with Imogene Heowener, and at the close of the service during the singing of "Softly and Tenderly," Sister Evie approached us and asked whether we had been saved. "No," we replied and she said, "Well that's very bad, because if you die tonight, you will burn in the fires of hell forever." Sis, along with Imogene, thought that was a fate too horrible to contemplate, agreed to join the church and went up front, over my admonition that Mom would be really mad. I was more concerned about the wrath of Mom than the fires of hell and I tattled on Sis when we got home. The next day, Mom undid the joinder and forbade our going to any further services there.

A great sensation was caused when the two lady evangelists, Sisters Evie and Ruby, came to Duff to hold revivals. Many of the chronically unchurched attended, and members of the other churches came as well. Sister Evie preached fire and brimstone and didn't have an easy time of it. One evening, Dad, Lem Small, and Stanley Peach were seated in the "Amen corner." They had been imbibing pretty heavily and were singing the hymns with great gusto! Sister Evie approached Dad and asked, "Hugo, have you been drinking?" to which he replied, "No, Ma'am." She turned to Lemuel and asked the same question to which he replied, "No Ma'am." She then asked Stanley, who croaked, "Yes, Sir" and the churchhouse rang with laughter.

Alex Lemond entered Wayne's store one day, and Wayne said, "Well doggone, here is the old devil himself." Alex responded, "In person." Wayne grinned and said, "Alex, tell us how this came about, you gettin' that handle." "Well, I went to church the other evenin' with the old lady to hear those lady preachers and when the big fat gal preacher came around glad-handin' the people, she came up greetin' me, so I thought I would just ask her a couple of things, and I said, 'Say, how can you get up there and preach when the Bible says a woman should keep silent in church?'" Alex went on, "Boys, I'm tellin' you she gave me a hard, mean look and didn't answer at all. She whirled, and went right up to the pulpit, as it was time to start anyway, and turnin' around, she threw her arms in the air and shouted, 'Folks, I want you to know that I've just met the old Devil face to face and he's sittin' right there.' She pointed straight at me. And she went right on and preached an entire sermon directed at me and my disbelief and how I had allowed the Devil to attack this poor preacher."

The Duffers thoroughly enjoyed Alex's set-to with the lady preacher. Alex, who had a great sense of humor about everything, including religion, said he was standing midway between the two churches one evening and they were both singing hymns. The Baptist church was singing "Will There Be Any Stars In My Crown," and the Christian church was singing, "No, Not One."

Our neighbor, Homer Osborn, married to Martha, one of the Lemond girls, who lived a half mile north of us, conducted church in the Odd Fellows hall for a number of years. He called his church, "The Church of God." Homer, whose hair was snow white, was a kind man, so kind he couldn't even discipline his horses when he worked the land bordering ours on the north. On many a Sunday morning, he stopped to pick me up where I would be waiting at our yard gate as he walked by, took me by the hand and we walked to the Odd Fellows Hall together.

My sister Kate and I and cousins Margie and Raymond Stapleton, formed a quartet and went with Homer to neighboring towns to sing hymns and gospel songs at services. Fortunately for us, we were not with him on a bright, cheerful Sunday morning in 1940, when he and a carload of other worshipers were on their way to church services in another community. I was at Spurlock's store and several of us noticed that a west-bound freight had stopped suddenly. Immediately, Bill Mayo rushed in to say that the freight had struck a car at the Duff crossing. We ran the block to the crossing in time to see townspeople removing the broken body of Homer Osborn from the smashed automobile. I saw, I can still see, his white hair stained with the bright red of his blood. Again, the town was cast into mourning. His death made me very sad.

SICKNESS, DEATH, AND DYING

Duff people were born at home and died at home. There was no hospital in the area, although doctors from Huntingburg and Velpen made house calls. All seven of the Songer children were born in the same bed in the same house. My oldest sister Katherine and I were banished to the upstairs when another birth was about to occur, but unknown to Mom and Dad, we crept halfway down the stairs so we could hear everything that happened. By the time my youngest sister Carol was about to be born, there was a hospital in Huntingburg, and Dr. McKinney and Dad were trying to talk Mom into going there. The argument raged back and forth until Mom finally declared, "All right, if the two of you are so all fired determined to go to the hospital, go ahead. I'm staying here and having this baby." There was very little they could do but go along with her, and after a couple of hours of birth pangs, we heard the wail of another Songer baby.

When someone was sick unto dying, neighbors brought food, did the family's chores, planted or tended the crops, and took turns sitting up all night with the afflicted so that family members could get some rest. In 1937, the year of the great flood, my sister Mary Ann, age three, became deathly ill. The doctor was summoned but high water prevented his arrival. Her condition worsened. That night, high fever sent her into convulsions and if she were to survive, it was essential to get her fever down. Someone suggested that they rub her body with alcohol, saying that its evaporation would have a cooling affect. There in the middle of the living room, dimly lit by the soft glow of two kerosene lamps, little Mary Ann was suspended in mid-air by five people, each holding a limb and her head, while they rubbed her entire body vigorously with alcohol in a desperate attempt to lower her temperature.

Dad, at one point, shoved back the lid of the top-loaded wood stove to throw in another chunk of wood and light from the fire lit up the room and Dad's face. Tears flowed down his fear-stricken face and dripped into the fire. I stood trembling, out to the side, next to the bed, terrified, transfixed. I could tell from the strained anxious faces of the adults that Mary Ann's life or death was hanging in the balance. Finally, in the wee hours of the morning, her fever broke. After daylight, the doctor arrived after having traveled part of the way by boat, and Mary Ann was on her way to recovery.

When folks died, they lay in state at home. I often went with Dad when he did his turn sitting up with the corpse. Two or more adults sat up together and talked in low tones about the deceased's merits and shortcomings, their cigarettes glowing in the dark. When Lincoln Hubster was expecting the arrival of the Grim Reaper, he told his survivors that he came into this world nude and he was going out the same way. They respected his wishes, and he lay there, uncovered to the waist, strong muscular arms folded across his hairy chest.

We dug their graves at the Payne and Mayo cemeteries with pick and shovel. Digging a hole six feet deep in that hard clay soil was a daunting task in the dry summer or in winter's frozen ground. Once, at Mayo cemetery, we dug into an ancient burial site and found only a few buttons and teeth. Truly, ashes to ashes and dust to dust.

Dad and I often went to Payne Cemetery where the pioneer ancestors of the hamlet sleep. That graveyard was started in 1840 when two young daughters of Elisha Payne wandered away from a sugar camp and got lost in the woods and perished of exposure. There, we visited the gravesites of Dad's infant brothers, Champ Clark and William Jennings Bryan, and of the Civil War veterans. Tennessee Pirtle is buried there, as is Stephen Lemond, who died on a hospital ship forty miles away on the Ohio River. His father, John B. Lemond, went after his body in a box wagon, the round trip consuming a total of four days. It was bitter cold and the body of his son was frozen. What a cold, sad trip that must have been. Hugo Lemond had saved one of the letters written by his Uncle Stephen a few months after he had entered the service. He wrote:

> *I want you all to write as soon as you get this little scribbled letter and I will try to write another. If it is too expensive for you to get stamps to mail your letters I will send you some when I get my money if I ever get any. So write soon and often—everyone of you write—even you Josephine. This is to all of you. Milton you had better write and that, soon. \s\ Stephen B. Lemond.*

Clearly, Stephen was homesick and wanted to hear from his folks.

Mayo Cemetery was started in 1879 when James Mayo was killed. His mules, hitched to a wagon, became frightened and ran away, throwing him out of the wagon and against a tree, breaking his neck and fracturing his skull, producing his death instantaneously. Mayo's eulogy, given by W.R. Osborn, a Civil War veteran, was eloquent in its statement of religious faith that existed at the time:

> *Uncle Jimmie, as all were wont to call him—alas! is no more. The icy hand of death was laid upon him when least expected and he has gone to reap that reward in a brighter world of bliss that is in store for God's people. With the trials and turmoils of this life he is done, and the immortal part, the Spirit that God gave, has been transported to Eternal Worlds on high, and joined in the song of the Redeemed sung by Seraphs around the throne of glory, and will continue to sing and worship the Great Creator throughout the ages of eternity.*

When Dad was an old man, we were at Mayo's graveyard one Memorial Day where nearly all of Dad's lifetime friends were buried and as he looked across the acre of tombstones, he mused, "This is where Duff is." Duff was a mile away, but I understood. It has been nearly twenty years since he rejoined them and when I go there, I am reminded of Gray's "Elegy Written in a Country Churchyard;"

Full many a gem of purest ray serene
The dark unfathomed caves of ocean bear:
Full many a flower is born to blush unseen,
and waste its sweetness on the desert air.

Far from the madding crowd's ignoble strife
Their sober wishes never learned to stray
Along the cool sequestered vale of life,
They kept the noiseless tenor of their way.

By the time I started to school, I thought I had a fairly good understanding of life. You were born, grew up, got married, went to work, had kids who grew up and got married, and soon you were a grandfather. You spent some good years on the store porch telling stories, and then you died. But I learned it did not always work this way.

Wilfred (Fuzz) Kays was my first hero. He was a big, strong, ruggedly handsome guy and one of the star players on the Duff Indians baseball team. He lived with his sister Nellie and her husband, Gilbert Sunderman, who used his steam engine to power the saw mill he ran in winter. Fuzz worked for him, and was using a cut-off saw to cut slab wood into stove lengths. In one brief moment of inattention, he lost two fingers to the saw.

He was taken to the doctor who bandaged the hand but neglected to administer a tetanus shot. We thought Fuzz was well on his way to recovery, but soon he became deathly sick. The doctor was summoned and the dread diagnosis, lock-jaw, spread through the community. For a week or more he lay, feverish and delirious, unable to eat through clenched teeth. Then, unbelievably, he died and the community was cast into mourning at the loss of this young hero. Fuzz was buried at the foot of a giant oak tree in Mayo cemetery. Many times over the years, I visited his grave site, pondering the loss and lessons learned. When I wish to relive the experience of his final days, I read Robert Frost's poem, "OUT, OUT—," which seems to chronicle Fuzz's experience. In his poem, Frost tells of a young man who lost a hand to a buzz saw which he was using to cut stove-length sticks of wood:

He saw all spoiled. "Don't let him cut my hand off
The doctor, when he comes. Don't let him sister!"
So. But the hand was gone already.
The doctor put him in the dark of ether.
He lay and puffed his lips out with his breath.
And then—the watcher at his pulse took fright.
No one believed. They listened at his heart.
Little—less—nothing—and that ended it.
No more to build on there. And they, since they
Were not the one dead, turned to their affairs.

FROSTY JONES

After Fuzz Kays, Forrest (Frosty) Jones was my next great hero. Frosty's father was in an institution, leaving his wife Ida the difficult task of raising the three children, Frosty, Nettie, and Ruth. Frosty went to live with Bill Forston, a relative north of Duff, where he was to earn his keep by working on the farm. Forston was brutal to Frosty, and every time something went wrong or got broken, Bill blamed Frosty and gave him a beating. One day the tongue of the hay rake was broken when a horse stepped on it, and the customary beating resulted. This time, a neighbor saw what happened and told Forston that if he ever laid a hand on Frosty again, he would kill him.

That ended the beatings, but Frosty soon left anyway and lived and worked for Robert Small on the farm. Shortly thereafter, Frosty got into a fight with another boy who was badly cut, so at the age of fifteen, Frosty ran away to St. Louis where he got a job working on the railroad. Frosty, who had only five years of schooling, learned a lot in the school of hard knocks, and after a few years, returned to Duff, bought an old truck, and began hauling products for local manufacturers. His trucking business soon grew to a fleet of five trucks, called "Jones Fast Freight." It looked like Frosty was on his way to great things, and then came the Great Depression. Hauls became fewer and fewer and soon, Frosty, like many other men, had time on his hands.

One cold, blustery, winter day, Frosty, Kelso Hall, and Noble Hochmeister were loafing at Wayne Hall's store. Suddenly, the door flew open and in walked Sheriff Kendall, who looked like he really meant business. "Boys," he said, "I have just been informed by the Pike County sheriff that he is looking for two men, Corn and Aldridge, who are wanted for a bunch of thefts and burglaries. He chased them across the Pike County line into Dubois County and the word is they're holed up at Anna Russell's house. I'm gonna deputize you three men to help me hunt them down."

He swore in Frosty and the other two men and armed them with .38 revolvers and .30 caliber rifles. When the men left Wayne's store, it began snowing hard, so they decided to go to the Russell home to try to pick up the trail of the fugitives. The newly formed posse met two men on the road they didn't know and after talking it over, decided they were Corn and Aldridge. So they turned around and started after them. After tracking them for a while, they spotted them walking across a snowy field and the posse yelled for them to stop. The men started running and the posse began firing wildly. The men kept running. Frosty placed his rifle on a fence post and took careful aim. The bullet kicked up snow between the two men. Corn and Aldridge surrendered.

Practical jokes were among our greatest forms of entertainment, and Frosty played a lead role in one that was talked about on the store porches for years. It was called the "Great Chicken Roast." One Saturday night, Menlo Collins, Frank Small, Otho Brewster, Fuzz Kays and Cletus Gambill were at loose ends in Spurlock's store. Charlie was closing the store early—he and wife Minnie and daughters Dorothy and Lucille were going visiting for the evening and as luck would have it, none of the other young girls were at home that evening either.

The boys had no car, nor any money. Prospects for any fun that Saturday evening were grim indeed! Suddenly Otho spoke up and said: "Let's have a chicken roast!" That sounded like a great idea and as they walked west on the railroad track, they began to plan. Near Steineker's crossing, the banks are high on each side of the track and would hide their fire. Fuzz and Cletus volunteered to go to Jim Collins place and grab a few unlucky chickens off the roost while the others gathered wood and built a fire. Fuzz and Cletus left but not for chickens. Instead, they went back to Duff and got Frosty Jones whose services they needed for a plot to throw a wild scare on the would-be chicken eaters in the railroad cut. Frosty went back with them but lagged behind a little.

It was a moonlight night, and when they approached with a gunny sack over Fuzz' shoulder, silhouetted against the moonlit sky, Otho called out: "Got the chickens?" to which Frosty replied, imitating Jim Collins' voice, "I'll show you what I got for chicken thieves!" and fired two rounds from his double barrel shotgun. Fuzz and Cletus screamed and fell to the ground. The boys around the fire were frozen in place momentarily, and then fled for their lives, as Frosty ranted in Jim Collins' voice and fired a couple more rounds through the trees.

All the boys took a roundabout way home and went straight to bed. They spent a sleepless night as they visualized poor old Fuzz and Cletus lying dead there in the field. A couple of the boys stayed home for a few days, but Frank Small decided to walk to Duff to see what the fallout was from the shooting. As luck would have it, along came Jim Collins in his box wagon and offered Frank a ride to Duff. He climbed aboard and noticed immediately that Jim was cheerful, even humming a tune, very unusual behavior for a man who had just shot two people the night before. He asked Jim if he had heard any shots last night and Jim replied that he had—down toward the cut in the railroad track, but he didn't know who did the shooting or what it was all about. Frank began to smell a rat before they arrived at Wayne's store, and when he saw Fuzz and Cletus sitting there grinning, his suspicions were confirmed. When the group found out how they had been duped, there were some hard feelings for a while. Frank Small offered to whip all their asses and opined that they were all a bunch of sons-a-bitches and somehow they were going to pay. Among all the practical jokes ever staged in Duff, this one deserved first prize!

In 1927, something occurred that was to shape Frosty's direction and ambition for the rest of his life—Charles Lindbergh's solo flight across the Atlantic. Soon, Frosty had his first plane ride. Then he scraped the money together to take flying lessons. Flying, and Frosty's cocky, brash attitude were a perfect match—and Frosty knew what he wanted to do for the rest of his life. He went to Ohio to purchase his

Forrest (Frosty) Jones, Ora Songer, flyers.

first airplane. His return was delayed, and it was after dark when he arrived. He buzzed his home and when his wife Merle emerged from their home, he dropped a note tied to a rock instructing her to have several people drive their cars to the landing strip on a local farm and shine their lights on the grass runway. In order to avoid two stumps that remained on the landing strip, he asked Merle to have a man stand on each of them. Frosty brought his new airplane in.

He used various pastures around Duff to take off and land, selling rides to support his new hobby. Every spring when the farmer plowed the field or turned his cows loose, Frosty had to look for a new landing strip. Tiring of this, Frosty got several investors together who were also interested in flying and they purchased land near Huntingburg for an airport. (That small dirt strip has evolved into a modern airport that will accommodate jet aircraft.)

Nearly every time Frosty went flying, he would "buzz" Duff, raking his wheels through the tops of the giant elm trees that grew along the alley. As soon as he appeared, I ran onto the baseball field and waved my arms, and Frosty flew so low that I "bit the dust." He climbed to 5000 feet and did a tailspin, or "falling leaf," and inside and outside loops, all performed for us as we sat transfixed on Wayne Hall's store porch. He began barnstorming at county fairs and similar public events, doing acrobatics—tailspins, barrel rolls, and inside and outside loops, and if there was a landing strip nearby, gave rides for a fee. Frosty was now making a living at what he loved doing—flying.

In 1940, he was in Florida for a national acrobatics event, flying an airplane owned by a Miami flying service. Frosty had just completed his acrobatics and as he flew inverted, down low over the field, he suddenly flipped the airplane right side up and set it down on the runway. An army general was so impressed with this bit of flying that he asked to meet him. They hit it off, and Frosty was hired to train army pilots. Later, after the war started, Frosty flew war materiel from the United States to Africa, via Puerto Rico and South America. Lacking navigational equipment, the pilots used dead reckoning to find their destination. The C-46s they flew cruised at about one hundred-eighty knots and were not equipped for water landings. If they went down, that was it. On one occasion, they were warned that they might encounter some headwind. There was a crew of three—pilot, co-pilot, and navigator.

The young college-trained navigator called out his estimate of where they were at given intervals, and as they neared what they believed was the halfway point, the so-called point of no return, the location given by the navigator indicated they had flown only twenty miles during the last hour.

Frosty usually trusted his own instincts and wasn't sure he could trust the college boy with little flying experience. A decision had to be made fast. He decided to trust the young navigator, and turn around and go back to South America. They streaked back at nearly four hundred miles an hour. After landing, they learned they had been flying into a two hundred mph headwind. Frosty said they soon learned they had better gain altitude before leaving the land mass of South America, or German submarines would take pot-shots at them.

After the war, Frosty flew jets for Eastern Airlines, eventually becoming their senior pilot. All this on five years of formal education. But Frosty was a great seat-of-the-pants flier, and on a few occasions during his career, he felt that his natural flying ability saved his passengers and plane. On a trip from Chicago to Miami, Frosty was flying a Lockheed Electra, his favorite airplane, when the plane was struck by lightning, causing the generator to short out. All flight indicators were disabled except altimeter and compass "ball and needle." Frosty flew the airplane in solid overcast using only basic instruments, flashlight and wristwatch. When they broke through the ceiling at three hundred feet, they were directly above the Miami Airport.

Another time, a DC-3 he was flying iced up and he was unable to clear the mountains in West Virginia because of the heavy load of ice that was hanging a foot out on the hubs of the propellers. Even with throttles wide open, the plane was descending three hundred feet per minute. Frosty and his crew and passengers were reported down by regional traffic control, but he had turned north toward Cleveland. When they got close, the stub antenna enabled him to make contact with the tower. At four hundred feet they broke out of the icy clouds. It was snowing now with visibility obscured, so Frosty broke open both side windows so they might see familiar landmarks. At last, the co-pilot recognized a building, Frosty changed course, and slammed the crippled plane down on the runway at full power. He was a great flyer and a hero to many, our Duff boy, Frosty Jones.

DUFF SCHOOL

Duff School, located directly across the road from the Songer homeplace, was a typical one-room school, with a single large classroom and an anteroom where the children hung their coats and their drinking cups and kept their lunch buckets. It was located on an acre of land, just large enough to accommodate our games. Each morning before school started, and at recess and noon, we played a baseball game called "move-up." When the batter made an out, he or she went to the outfield and rotated positions until he was again, "in-bats." Some of the older and better players would remain in-bats a week or more.

We played crack-the-whip, red rover, fox and geese (when snow covered the ground), handy over, jump the rope, and marbles for keeps. Footpaths ran in every direction from the school, some of them a mile or two in length. The Smith kids walked a mile or more, crossed fences over stiles at two locations, and set rabbit traps along the way to provide food for the family table. Raymond and Margie Stapleton walked the railroad track for two miles from their home west of Duff, and in the spring, the Sunderman and Davis children were sure to come part way by boat across the high water.

Inside, the blackboard spanned the east wall, and there was an additional section of blackboard on the north and south walls. George Washington and Abraham Lincoln gazed down from the wall, and an American flag hung on its staff next to the organ. At the rear of the room was a bookcase, holding forty or fifty books, mostly by the great American authors—Longfellow, Hawthorne, Irving, Twain, Whitman, and Holmes, Hoosier authors Edward Eggleston and James Whitcomb Riley, and books of poetry, including verse by Shakespeare, Poe and Frost, among others.

I puzzled over Frost's poem, "The Pasture Spring," wondering how the description of such a commonplace event, could be so great. The volume I took down most often was a pictorial history of the great

Duff School

Galveston flood of 1900, which depicted hundreds of human bodies lying willy-nilly on the piles of debris. I thought about the vulnerability of human life, of the savagery of nature, and of the part God played in all of this.

A favorite story that I often read in that tiny school library at Duff, written by Nathaniel Hawthorne, called "The Great Stone Face," captured my attention and I never forgot it. It is the story of a boy, Ernest, who grows up in a valley, intrigued by the visage of a man's face on the side of a mountain and the prophecy that someday a great man will appear whose face will be identical to that of the great stone face on the mountain. All through his life, he gazed at the stone face until he felt that the face even smiled at him. Time after time, great men returned to the valley: a rich man, a great general, a poet, and in each instance the townspeople acclaimed that at last, the great man has appeared, only to have their hopes dashed. The boy grew into a man and into wisdom, his hair graying. People came from far and wide to be in the presence of his brilliance. The poet, who had himself journeyed to the valley to visit this great and humble man, realized that the face of Ernest himself, who had never left the valley, was the great stone face.

There were wooden school desks—some smaller for first graders, and large two-seaters for the 7th and 8th graders. Usually twenty-five or thirty children were spread over the eight grades, although the teachers often had students skip a grade if there were only one or two in a class and if they were capable of making the next grade. My fellow fifth graders were Bennie Borman and Margie Stapleton, which was fortunate for me, because they were excellent students and the three of us competed for the highest score. Sophia Arensman said we were the smartest kids she ever taught, and at the end of the fifth year, she promoted us to the seventh grade.

A recitation bench sat at the front of the room, next to the teacher's desk, and at this bench each class took its turn during the day to demonstrate how much they had learned. I spent most of each school day listening to each class recite and I knew the 8th grade material by

Duff School Student Body: Frt l-r: Richard Fark, Ben Borman, Raymond Stapleton, Buck Borman, Charlie Songer, Chalk Ermert, Buck Heowener, Lena Mae Smith, Detsyl Quackenbush, Audrey Summers, Margie Stapleton, Emagene Peach; 2nd-l: Harold Hilgeman, Dorothy Mae Osborn, Robert Smith, Cecil Smith, Bill Peach, Kenny Sunderman, Anna Mae Borman, Katherine Songer, Louanna Martin, Imogene Heowener; b-l: Sophie Arensman, teacher; Genevieve Brown, Kathleen Peach, Guthrie Sunderman, Chester Fark.

heart when I got there.

Both of my teachers were female. Sophia Arensman taught for six years and Huldah Cooper, one. Miss Arensman never married, which was expected of a teacher when she began teaching. She wore her wavy, graying hair in a bun, a duster to keep chalk dust off her clothing, and her watch as a brooch on her blouse. She was a wonderful teacher, a disciplinarian completely committed to her chosen profession, but she could not carry a tune in a tub.

Each morning, we had opening exercises, when we recited the pledge of allegiance, and sang "My Country 'Tis of Thee," "The Spanish Cavalier," or "My Bonnie Lies Over the Ocean," accompanied on the pump organ by my mother, who crossed the road each morning for opening exercises. Mom also helped Miss Arensman with the Christmas and last-day-of-school programs, when the school kids recited a poem or put on skits. The first graders were terrified when called upon—some refused to go up at all, even though they had rehearsed their short pieces at home for weeks, and others, coaxed to walk front and center, merely stood there, thumb in mouth, and then, seeing all eyes on them, ran terrified back to their mothers. My first Christmas recitation, while holding a large candy cane, was:

I bought Baby Sister a big stick of candy
It was only five cents—I had five cents handy
But Baby Sister can't eat candy you see
So she gave the candy to me.

Our proximity to the school dictated that the Songer family would be school janitors. Every year, before the school term, Dad mowed the schoolyard, which had grown up in weeds over the summer. We oiled the floor, washed the windows, polished the desks, and prepared Duff School for the fall term. When I was in the seventh grade, I became janitor. Every evening after school, I washed the blackboard, dusted the erasers by whacking them on the concrete front porch, swept the floor, and carried in two buckets of coal after banking the fire with coal slack for the night. In the morning, I stirred up the fire and added coal, so that the school room was toasty warm when the teacher arrived. In April, at the end of the school year, I was paid for the entire term, twenty four dollars.

A spectacular incident known as "The Great Coal Bucket Defacation," occurred before I started to school, but the infamy of the incident lived on for many years. My friend Gobby Collins was there and I will let him tell the story in his own words:

> *Chester (Check) Brown was a Duff boy who managed to go to Oakland City College and earn a teaching certificate in a nine months course. We locals were proud of him when he was hired to teach at Duff school, but he was really a "prophet not without honor, except in his own country." He wasn't Mr. Brown, just our old friend Check. However, he did his teaching job well and at the end of the term, wrote witty sayings on our report cards. Mine said that I had passed "by the skin of my teeth." Another student's said they had passed by a "hair's breadth."*
>
> *Elmer (Dutch) Ermert didn't appreciate that he had made it "by the flap of a gnat's wing." So in the beginning of school the next fall, Dutch decided that he would bring this brash young teacher down a peg or two. No one knew what Dutch had in mind, but disaster befell the school room one morning a few days after the start of school, and all of the kids had an idea as to who was the instigator of that foul plot. When Check arrived at school that fateful morning, unlocked the door and stepped inside, followed by a bevy of students, everyone grabbed their noses and yelled, "PHEW" in chorus. Check gasped for air and pushed the kids back as he bravely entered the class room. "Something's rotten in here," opined our brave teacher, and he strode purposefully around the room. Finally he homed in on the source of the stench and stirred around a bit in the coal bucket, which really sent the aroma flying throughout the room.*

Peering into the coal bucket, Check spied several large defecates lying there in innocent repose. Grabbing the coal bucket, he hurled the whole blamed mess into the fire, thinking to burn away the gaseous odor that befouled the room. However, the hot coals accentuated the stench, and reams of awfulness rent even the atmosphere thereabouts. Windows were thrown open and the children madly waved their jackets to drive the foul air away, and out of the building. Finally, Check said, "Probably, there are some that think this to be funny, but I don't think so, and I will get to the bottom of this devilish plot and the culprit will be very sorry that he or she ever came up with such an idea. In fact, I plan to have the guilty party spend some part of every day sitting in the outhouse and enjoying the odors that he wanted to share with the rest of us—then he can have them all to himself." Well, supposed innocents were passed by, but those easily suspect were called before Mr. Brown's court and questioned vigorously, haloes floated above the heads of those who were ordinarily guilty of pranks and rotten deeds. No one knew anything about this foul "lower than a skunk's belly, crude, degrading, besmirching, nasty, unheard-of deed," as Check stated it, and what was more, they said they wouldn't even think of doing such a pitiful, spiteful, ornery lack-of-character act! Nobody, including teacher, believed them, for someone had most assuredly done the dastardly deed. So the inquisition went on and on every day for a long time, but the truth evaded Mr. Brown's court. And it has unto this very day! If Dutch was guilty, no one could prove it. He wouldn't admit it and neither would his cohorts. So none us, save one, will ever know how the defecate found its way into the coal bucket. Some wanted Mr. Brown to question the girls, but he wouldn't stoop that low, so he said. So this case probably appears amongst the unsolved cases in the lower Indiana courts.

Miss Arensman had a rule that only one student could exit the school house at any given time to visit the outhouse. You were required to write your name on a slip of paper and hang it on a nail near the door to the anteroom. One morning, I began to feel a very strong urge to have a bowel movement but there was a note on the nail. I walked to the door and looked at the name on the slip. Lena May Smith. "Oh no," I groaned. When I turned to look at her desk and saw that it was empty I realized I was in deep trouble. Lena May was notorious for long outhouse visits (actually, she spent time on the playground). She stayed and stayed. I tried thinking of something else, concentrating on my studies, all to no avail. Suddenly, I filled my pants. Horrified, I noticed that I was getting sidelong glances from those sitting near me, so I bolted from the room, crossed the road and went home. I changed clothes but refused to return to school unless Mom accompanied me to explain the situation. Surprisingly, none of my schoolmates ever commented on the situation.

Gobby tells the story that Ruth Jones once saved Leoda Quackenbush a spanking at the hands of the teacher, Tibby Robinson. Tibby, in an effort to teach the children a lesson about how we should help those who are in distress, posed a question that he wanted the class to think about and respond to the next day. The question was, "What should you do if a man's car broke down in front of your house and he asked you for help?" Leoda talked to her dad, Jimmy Quackenbush about it and Jimmy thought it was a dumb question, so he told Leoda to say: "Give him a dose of castor oil and send him on his way quick!" When she gave that answer the next morning, Tibby thought she was being a smart-aleck and threatened to spank her. Ruth spoke up and explained that Leoda's father Jimmy told her to say that. Tibby relented.

We had a dog, Nipper, who looked like and was named after the small black and white dog shown in RCA Victor ads, with an ear cocked, sitting in front of a victrola. Nipper disappeared, and for a week we combed the area asking neighbors whether they had seen him. No one had. One day during recess at school, someone yelled, "Nipper is back." Sure enough, there he was, across the road from the school, lying in front of our yard gate. As we approached, we could see that something was dreadfully wrong. He was listless and foaming at the mouth. From past experience, we were certain that Nipper was "mad." Miss Arensman rang the bell and ordered everyone into the schoolhouse and then sent the oldest student, Earl Smith, to tell Dad about Nipper. Earl surely knew about mad dogs and the danger they presented. A bite from a rabid dog could kill you unless you could get the very painful anti-rabies shots. But rather than use the barnlot gate or cross the fence away from where Nipper lay, Earl crossed the road, walking directly toward the yard gate and fearlessly stepped over the prone body of the dog. Fortunately for Earl, Nipper was too sick to react. Dad had no choice but to shoot Nipper. We buried him with full honors.

The school caught on fire one afternoon when school was not in session. Elmer "Dutch" Ermert saw the smoke coming from the belfry and came running, grabbed a ladder from our place, and got into the space over the anteroom. A built-in ladder led from there into the belfry, where the fire burned, and by this time, enough people had arrived to form a bucket brigade from the school house well. Soon, the fire was extinguished with only minor damage to the belfry. The only rational theory for the cause of the blaze was that a nesting bird had carried a smoldering cigarette butt into her nest in the belfry. Like Gobby Collins, I cannot help but wax sentimental about those days at Duff school. But Gobby said it best:

> *The old school bell still rings as I think of those days long past, its message calling on a bright fall day—come and learn, come and learn. And learn we did from those great mentors that guided our early years—Hilton (Tibby) Robinson, Sophia Arensman, and Hulda Cooper. We thought the best years of our lives were still to come, but as I look back these were golden years, to be forever treasured in our storehouse of memories, to be drawn out on occasion and savored with pleasure and enjoyment, for it was that part of our lives that molded into us the character attributes that pointed us into the world, from that little one room school in a quiet country village nestled in the hills and valleys of southern Indiana.*

Last day of school dinner, Duff School, 1937-38.

THE DUFF INDIANS

Since shortly after the turn of the century, Duff had a baseball team called the Duff Indians. The team that took the field during the 1920s, featuring the pitching and hitting of Tom Stapleton, Jess Hall, and Fuzz Kays, was a tough one which finished each season with a winning record and held its own with teams from much larger towns. They played successfully into the 1930s when they reached their prime, but lost the heart to continue after the death of Fuzz Kays. Something like that is a life-changing experience. For several years, Duff had no team.

In 1943, when some of us had grown large enough to play, we again fielded a team. Several Duff boys were in the service, and we were short of players so the team consisted of boys too young and men too old to go to war, and a few farmers who had deferments. Our playing field was located in Hugo Lemond's pasture field across the road from Wayne Hall's store. The diamond was bereft of grass and Hugo's cattle loved lolling around in the dust on the baseball diamond. Before every home game, we removed several dozen cow piles with broad scoop shovels that were a necessary part of our equipment. Then we dragged the diamond, sometimes carelessly. Once a Jasper batsman in an effort to stretch a double into a triple made a beautiful hook slide into a cowpile that had been overlooked, which he mistook for third base. He was tagged out, which compounded his embarrassment as he attempted to shake off the cow manure that extended from his socks to his cap. The Indians' equipment was contained in a green army duffel bag that sat just inside the door of Wayne Hall's store. There was the catcher's gear, a few bats, half a dozen scruffy baseballs and a catcher's mitt. Every evening in summer, we played catch in the road and if Lewis Hochmeister was around, we retired to the

Duff Indians

Frt-l: Arnie Sunderman, Harold Hilgeman, Bill Rummel, Wilfred Rauscher, Carl Hilgeman; Bk-l: Jack Small, Dick Hubster, Raymond Stapleton, Harold Sunderman, Alan Stilwell.

baseball diamond across the road and fence where Lewis hit fly balls until it was too dark to see.

I became adept at catching fly balls and was fully aware of the audience on the store porch who had nothing better to do than watch me chase fly balls. I started playing regularly when I was sixteen. We were playing Gentryville one Sunday and Wayne Hall bet a Gentryville fan five dollars on the outcome of the game. That day, I hit my first home run. The left field fence was short, not more than three hundred feet. Across the fence was the road and beyond that Wayne Hall's residence. The ball landed in the road, and took a high bounce through Wayne's upstairs window. Wayne won the bet but the new window pane cost a dollar so he netted only four dollars from his bet.

Obtaining transportation for players and fans to games away from home was a major undertaking, what with the dearth of cars and gas rationing. As a result, we often rode in Red Maxey's tankage truck, usually called the "dead truck," which Red used during the week to pick up dead animals from local farms to be made into glue and fertilizer. Red's real name was Burvis, and he had brothers Pervis, Pearl and Pearless. Red hosed out the truck before hauling the team on Sunday, but it was not a pleasant ride. Everything had a greasy, oily feel and us farm boys knew where it came from. We had to learn to live with the ragging comments from players and fans of neighboring towns when we rolled in with the name "Farmers Tankage Company" emblazoned on the side of the truck.

The Duff baseball field has the all-time record in the history of the game for sponsoring the longest home run. A St. Henry batsman hit a long drive to deep center field. Clearing the fence, the ball crossed another small field between the fence and the railroad track, and finally settled into a carload of coal, which was part of a west bound freight train. The baseball didn't hit the ground until the coal was dumped in a St. Louis coalyard a hundred and eighty miles away.

Paulie Davis had been a Golden Gloves boxer in the middleweight class in Evansville, Indiana, and looked the part. Standing at 5′9″, and weighing about one hundred-fifty, he was narrow at the hips, with muscular arms and upper body. I never knew Paulie to pick a fight, but because of his build and reputation, toughs hanging around the bars near the depot in Huntingburg often tried to pick fights with him. Paulie was not one to turn them down. In the restroom at Greener's Cafe, someone threw a punch at Paulie and Paulie retaliated with a hard right. He missed and drove his fist through the plywood wall. I know—I went there to see it.

Occasionally, Paulie donned boxing gloves and sparred with the boys, including myself, in front of Wayne Hall's store. When Guthrie Sunderman returned home from the service with a reputation as a street fighter, I promoted a match between Guthrie and Paulie. They sparred around a while, but pretty soon their competitive juices began flowing and they went after each other.

Paulie was one of the Duff Indians' best pitchers. In addition to his boxing and baseball talent, he picked guitar. One summer afternoon, Paulie and Dad iced down a tub of beer, gathered some singers and had a hoedown in our front yard. My brother Jim was learning to play guitar and he, along with Harold Gearner on the fiddle, seconded Paulie all afternoon.

For a time, Paulie had a guitar which he called Stella. Stella, we all assumed, was a past love for whom Paulie still felt considerable passion. One afternoon, we were having a good old time. Paulie, who was sitting on a keg, was playing with particular skill and energy, embracing his guitar and smiling as he sang. The lyrics told of unrequited love—love of overwhelming intensity, but also a frustrating love, one in which loyalty and commitment was not returned. As the song went on, a cloud seemed to cross Paulie's face. His smiling visage became a scowl, and then one of anger. Suddenly, and without a word, Paulie stood up, smashed his guitar over the tailgate of a nearby pickup truck, and went home. Clearly, Stella 'done him wrong.'

Like many other Duffers, including my dad, Paulie was a drinker, and a pal of the Gearner brothers, Ben and Harold. He played music and drank with Harold, and went regularly with Ben Gearner on his

Paulie Davis and wife, Julie (Spitzer).

monthly trip to Huntingburg after Ben's pension check arrived. After one such binge, Harold and Paulie were on Wayne's store porch in the wee hours of the morning, drunk and without cigarettes. They broke into Wayne's store and stole some. They were caught, convicted of burglary, and sentenced to two years in prison, returning home after serving one and a half. During his stint in prison, Paulie had learned to cut hair, and became the community barber. One Sunday morning, we were getting ready for a home baseball game. Paulie was supposed to pitch, but was nowhere to be found. We inquired of his family and friends, searched the town, and couldn't find Paulie. Finally, I looked in Wayne Hall's coal shed and there he was, asleep on the coal, where he had spent the night. Hung over, he looked and felt like hell of course, but we roused him, cleaned off the coal dust, and plied him with coffee. Soon, his energy began flowing again, and he pitched an outstanding game that afternoon.

Paulie's growing-up years in Evansville were not happy ones due to his dad's excessive drinking, so in his teen years, he began spending time with his Uncle Coon Spitzer, a German farmer living a mile east of Duff. Coon's daughter Julie and her husband Emil Sunderman lived with Coon, and divorced in 1929. Thereafter, Julie and Paulie were together a lot, and in 1936, Paulie and Julie had twin sons, Ronald and Donald. Just before the birth of their daughter, Beverly, in 1938, Paulie and Julie married.

It was late winter of 1954 when I last spent time with Paulie, just after I had been discharged from the army. I was preparing to go south for spring training, and Paulie volunteered to pitch baseball to me for some batting practice. We continued this over several days in a field between our barn and the town of Duff. When I enrolled at Indiana University that fall, my trips to Duff became rare, and I lost track of Paulie. One crisp fall evening, with stars hanging in clusters over the Spitzer farm, near the confluence of Elk Creek and the Patoka river, Paulie was home with his family. He stepped out of the house, as he was often wont to do, to get a breath of fresh air, or to check on the animals in the barn. After an hour went by and Paulie didn't return to the house, Julie became concerned, and searched the barn and surrounding premises the best she could. The next morning, she notified her extended family and neighbors of his disappearance, and inquired of everyone in the Duff area who spent time with Paulie concerning his whereabouts. The sheriff was notified and search parties extended the search beyond the Spitzer farm—all without success. Finally, Julie and the children had to accept the fact that Paulie had disappeared without a trace.

The following spring, son Ronnie was discing down a field of weeds on some bottom ground near Elk Creek. Something flashed white beneath the disc. He stopped the tractor and looked more closely. He could see that it was a skull and he thought immediately of his missing father. He unhooked the disc and sped to the farmhouse to tell his mother. The sheriff and coroner were notified and came immediately and examined the remains. Paulie's billfold, containing his hunting license and cash, was found in the trouser pocket. The circumstances of his death will forever remain a mystery.

DUFFERS AT PLAY

Above Charlie Spurlock's store was the Odd Fellows Hall. The fraternal organization had fallen into disrepair during my lifetime, but in a small locked room over the stairs was a stuffed goat, Roman cloaks, spears, and other paraphernalia used in their initiation ceremonies. Across the south side of the hall was a riser, and a wire spanning the room across the riser held the curtains. This served as a stage. All sorts of community events were staged in the hall. There were Christmas programs, plays, medicine man shows, and church services. Gobby Collins recalled a Christmas program in the 1920s:

The village Christmas celebration would once again be held in the I.O.O.F. Hall. A stage had been built for a Christmas play; school kids were to recite their Christmas pieces, and sing Christmas carols. Even a four-year-old boy named Gobby was pushed into performing by Flora Hall. She had taught him a little piece to recite.

I'm Mama's little darling
And Papa's little pet
I fell into the washtub
And got my britches wet.

I was wildly applauded by my family who were the only ones who could understand my frightened mumblings! The hall was full of villagers who came to the gathering, snow covered and with happy anticipation. They filtered away in their Model Ts and horses and buggies, and even a one horse drawn sleigh. So we went home to our feather beds to sleep away the night while Santa struggled down our chimneys to leave our presents before the fire.

One evening, as our family was anticipating a trip to the Odd Fellows Hall for a medicine man show and was preparing to leave home, heat from a lamp chimney ignited a curtain covering the kitchen cupboard and the fire blazed suddenly, igniting paper lining the cupboard shelves and scorching the wood. Dad grabbed the curtain with his bare hands, ripped it from the cupboard, threw it down and stomped it out. After a few minutes, we left on foot for the hall, never bothering to lock the doors—in fact, the kitchen door to the outside couldn't be locked. The hall was nearly packed when we arrived and the place was abuzz with anticipation of the big show. The medicine man did a few magic tricks—made things disappear and reappear. Bending a steel rod into a U shape and then straightening it again, he challenged the strong men in the house to duplicate the feat, which none of them could. He had enlisted four-year-old, curly-headed Marvin Stapleton to be his assistant, and at the point the medicine man was chiding the men in the audience for their inability to bend the rod, young Marvin came walking out from a side curtain with a second rod, the one he had bent double. With a bit of sleight-of-hand, the medicine man had switched rods. He was almost hooted out of the hall, but the manner in which his fake strong man act was revealed worked so well, he surely made it part of his act. Perhaps it already was.

After the house settled down, he asked for a volunteer who would allow water to be removed from his brain. Elmer Ermert volunteered. He had Elmer seated on stage and with a flourish, lay out his equipment—a hose, a funnel, and a glass jar. After wrapping a towel around Elmer's head, he stuck the hose into the cloth (and supposedly into Elmer's skull) and soon water was pouring through the hose into the jar. Not much of an act, you say, but everyone enjoyed the amazing feat, except Carrie Ermert, who didn't believe the medicine man should have removed the water from Elmer's brain.

The son of the medicine man, whom he called "Tickle Britches," became sweet on Sallie Sunderman during the few days they were in town, even walked her home one evening, and when he sang a song as part of the entertainment that mentioned "My Sallie," the audience howled. Not very funny, you say, but humor was not required to be sexy, sophisticated, or subtle.

Finally, it was time for that for which he came, which was to sell medicine. He had all kinds of pills and elixirs, and the one I remember best were the herbs he sold for the treatment of rheumatism. Dad always had trouble with his knees, and the medicine man said the herbs came from the Orient, and were used by Oriental physicians to treat rheumatism. He instructed Dad to soak the herbs in water for a week and then drink the liquid. As instructed, Dad put the entire dose in a glass jar and placed the jar on a table in the back kitchen. Daily, I watched the progress of the liquid concoction. Bits and pieces of herbs swirled around, the liquid turned green, and as it developed into a horrible looking mess, I wondered how Dad could ever drink it! After the prescribed week had passed, Dad took a look at it and decided it was "ripe." He drank it down and within a few days swore that his rheumatism had disappeared.

A group of Duffers got together and put on plays in the hall. Nellie Sunderman, Annie Stapleton, Ruth Jones, Jeanette Rauscher, Lucille Spurlock, Emerald Gambill, Selma Ermert, Chester Brown, Elmer and Lee Lemond, and Fuzz Kays, were cast members in a tear-jerker called "An Old Fashioned Mother." Its central theme concerned a widowed mother with a wayward son. The son, who was constantly making life more difficult for his poor, downtrodden mother, finally did the ultimate bad deed of running away with her life savings. He was gone for many years during which she had to depend upon the kindness of friends and neighbors for a living. Toward the end, just as she was about to go to the poorhouse, with a horse and buggy waiting to take her there, the wayward son came home, rich and respected, just in time to save his poor mother from the poorhouse! The house was full, and as the curtain closed, there was sobbing and blowing of

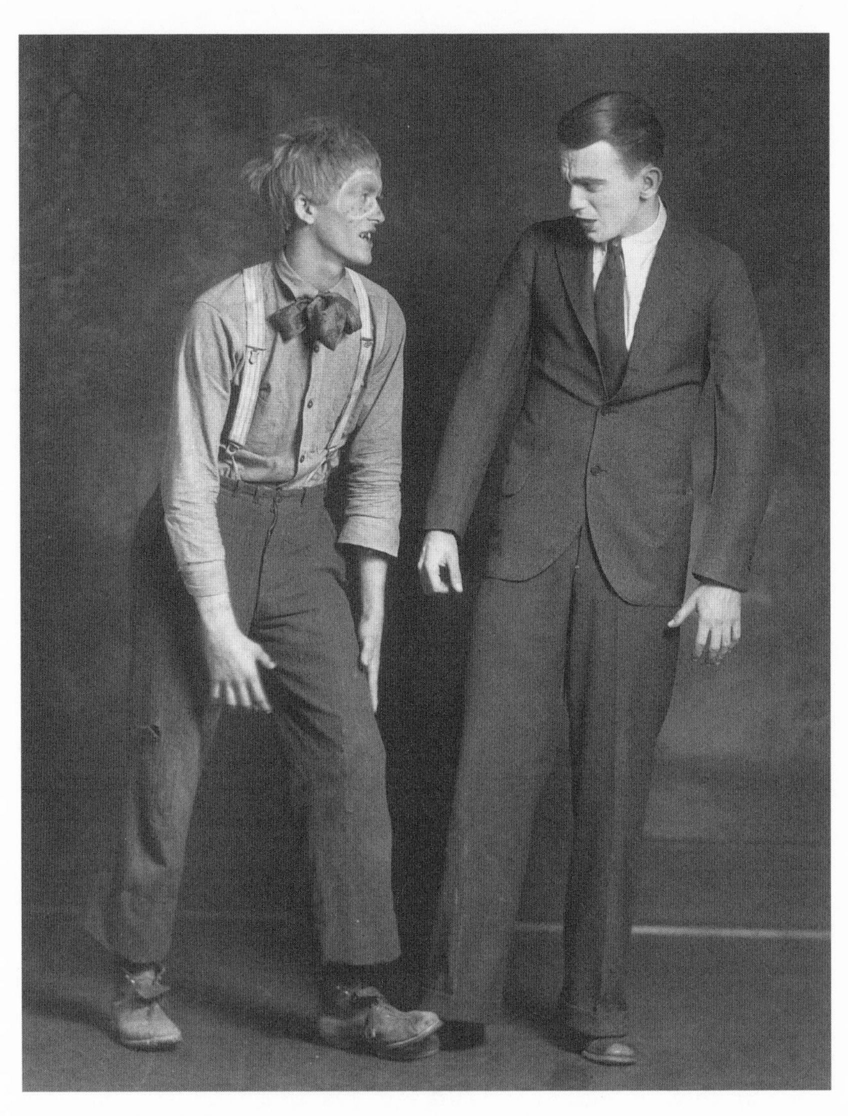

Lee Lemond and Chester Brown as actors.

noses as the audience experienced the son's redemption. In particular, Robert Small seemed carried away by the emotion of the play's ending.

Chester Brown liked performing so much that he decided to go to New York and take acting lessons. After a few months, he despaired of becoming successful there, so he returned to Duff and brought two New York show girls (and their mother) with him. They all stayed at the Brown residence, where to Mrs. Brown's dismay, the linoleum-covered kitchen floor became pitted from tap dance rehearsals, and she was required to prepare meals for the three adult guests. The girls created a sensation at the Odd Fellows Hall because Duffers had never known anyone from New York before, especially show girls. Soon, the shows outgrew the hall, so Chester and Lee Lemond formed the Brown and Baker tent show and toured surrounding towns under that name. A recitation that was a regular part of Chester's act was "The Face on the Bar-room Floor." Taking a cue from the medicine man, Chester had his younger brother Eugene and Don Peach hawk medicine and sundries during intermission.

For the store porch boys, the only boring time in Duff was Sunday afternoon. The stores closed at noon, and if there was no baseball game, or if the game was away from home, and we could not get a ride to follow the team, we were at loose ends. On a rainy day we often went to the covered bridges, Postlethwaite or Kessner, where we were in the dry and could climb around in the superstructure and read the carvings made in the 1880s and 90s by other boys on rainy days. Across the Postlethewaite covered bridge in Pike County was our favorite swimming hole, the rock quarry. There were very few places to swim before the bulldozer—it took a long time to dig a pond or lake with a team of horses and a slip scraper. The rock quarry was formed when a steam shovel had been used to excavate limestone which was to be pulverized into small rock for paving roads. An earthen ramp once used by trucks to haul rock from the quarry bed was our entry into the quarry after it filled with water, and allowed us to drive into the water a few feet to wash cars. We all knew the depth of the water off the ramp, but one day Arnie Sunderman made a misstep and backed into deep water. Arnie couldn't swim and would have drowned had Red Davis not thrown Arnie's bib overalls to him and pulled him to safety. Arnie, whom we called Jingles, was the first baseman of the Duff Indians. A few years later, he went to his barn loft, placed a 12-gauge shotgun muzzle in his mouth and blew the back of his head away allegedly because he feared being jailed for not having filed his income tax return. I think it was more complicated than that. In 1943, when Arnie was just a lad, he lost his father, Herman, and his sister Wilma, when both were killed at the Duff crossing by a westbound freight. Arnie never got over it.

The troubles of our proud and angry dust
Are from eternity and shall not fail.
Bear them we can, and if we can, we must.
Shoulder the sky, my lad, and drink your ale.
—A. E. Housman

There were a few places to fish. "The Pits," on the south side of the railroad track half way to Huntingburg, was a borrow pit which, as the name implies, was formed when dirt obtained from a field adjoining the railroad right-of-way was used to elevate the track surface above the wetland through which it passed. Strange fish were caught there, including gar, pondfish, and eels. Nearer Duff and also beside the railroad track was the Mill pond, shallow and full of lily pads, but well stocked with yellow-bellied catfish. West of Duff was the Factory pond, excavated early in the century with slip scrapers to provide water for the steam engine which powered the machinery in a canning factory. Alas, the factory burned in 1913 and was not rebuilt. Buck Heowener and I often took a sack of potatoes, a skillet, and our fishing lines to the Factory pond, and after building a fire and catching some small bluegill, we fried the potatoes and baked the fish in the hot coals. There on the dam in the shade of huge sycamore trees, as we ate our baked fish and fried potatoes, Buck would say

"Charlie, it doesn't get any better than this."

In summer, when the Patoka River was low, several men recruited a party of ten or twelve to go "hoggin." From past experience, they knew of places in the river, usually where trees had fallen in, where fish lay resting among the branches. We were equipped with a net, twenty or thirty feet long and three or four feet wide, with lead sinkers on one side which held the net on the bottom. When the net was in place around the "riffle," or fallen tree, several of us tended the net to insure that it extended from the bottom of the river to above water level, while others felt along the tree limbs and branches for fish. The Patoka water was the color of coffee with cream, and when they located a fish by feel, they ran their hands along it until they located the gills and mouth. (Oddly, the fish must have felt safe because they endured this without moving most of the time). After getting a secure hold, they simply lifted the fish out of the water and placed it in a gunny sack tended by others. Some of the fish were large, and you could guess their size before they cleared the water by the shaking of the arms and shoulders of the catchers when they got a firm hold on the fish. We often filled a couple of gunny sacks with this method of "fishing," the catch weighing perhaps one hundred-fifty pounds. They were primarily carp, buffalo, and catfish, with an occasional perch or eel. I was squeamish of the eels as they came squirming and twisting, snake-like, out of the water. When we got back to Duff, the fish were divided up, with everyone getting at least one preferred catfish.

Dad never participated in these group events. He preferred fishing or hunting alone, although he wasn't particularly good at either. He liked going to the woods, finding a good place to sit against a tree, where he waited for an occasional squirrel to wander within range. Once when I was small, I watched for him and when he came into view, I ran to meet him yelling, "Dad, did you get a squirrel?" He said, "No son, I saw one though—as a matter of fact, I saw three. I was sitting under a large den tree, that old beech up in the northeast corner of the woods, when a mother squirrel came out on a limb followed by two young squirrels. One of the young squirrels saw me and said 'Mommie, Mommie, there's a hunter!' The mother squirrel looked down and saw me and said: 'Oh, that's no hunter. That's Hugo Songer—he comes to this woods, and sits under this tree every year. He can't hit anything.' "

Sometimes a group of boys and girls walked the track to the Songer clay mine, where we climbed the tipple and entered the mine shaft, possible only if someone had the foresight to bring a flashlight or carbide miner's lamp. Adjoining the mine was a supply shed where the miners gathered at noon to eat dinner. Usually the shed was locked, but on one occasion we found it unlocked and upon entering, saw a cannister of carbide used to fuel the miner's lamps. Carbide mixed with water forms a gas, which when controlled and ignited, as in a miner's lamp, makes a bright flame. When carbide is mixed with water in a closed container, such as a glass jar with the lid screwed on tight, it becomes a bomb. All afternoon, we found discarded canning jars and made bombs. A contest developed over who could hold the jar the longest before it exploded. This was not an exact science and it was only a matter of time until someone held the jar too long. I don't know whether Ben Borman won or lost the game when a bomb he was prepared to throw exploded in his hand, causing a severe cut. Bombmaking and throwing ended for the day as we hurried down the track so that Ben could get his hand sewed up.

In 1940, the Duff Conservation Club built a club house on top of a hill at old Dufftown, one mile south of Duff. The storekeepers sponsored moving pictures, usually Charlie Chaplin or Laurel and Hardy, which were projected on an outdoor screen (a bedsheet stretched tight between two poles) on the hillside. There was a dance floor and the Club sponsored a dance nearly every Saturday night. Boys and girls my age were beginning to take an interest in each other, and often we teenagers held a square dance of our own. We stationed one of our younger members, usually Jesse Ahrens, near the juke box with a handful of nickels and she played "Under the Double Eagle" twenty or thirty times until we had our fill of square dancing!

SPURLOCK'S STORE

Charlie Spurlock and his wife Minnie owned and operated the store on the southeast corner of Duff. They had two daughters, Lucille and Dorothy, who made many a Duff swain swoon. Being people of some means, they had a piano in the parlor and a gasoline engine powered washing machine in the shed next to the house. The small engine had a flexible, metal exhaust hose about eight feet long with a bulb on the end, which was supposed to serve as a muffler, but you could hear the pop-pop-pop of the engine all over Duff. When Charlie fired up the engine on Monday morning, at the same time L.C. Brown started a similar apparatus for his wife Bertha up the block, the machines emitted so much smoke that a blue haze hung over the east end of Duff until noon.

The Spurlock store, larger than Wayne's, was a typical, rural, general merchandise store, featuring a large grocery and dry goods section in the main room, and a feed room in the back. The animal feed was contained in hundred pound cotton cloth sacks, in a variety of floral patterns that local housewives made into dresses and aprons for themselves and their daughters. The scrap material was saved for making quilts. Mom would point out the color pattern she wanted as I prepared to leave with my red wagon for a sack of chicken mash, and Woe is me! if I returned with the wrong one. There was a large concrete porch in front of the store with only a single bench for loafers because the store faced south and the hot afternoon sun discouraged lounging on the porch. Between the porch and the road was a hitching rack where farmers tied their teams. Inside, in the far left corner of the main room, was a large, coal-fired cannonball stove, around which were chairs and benches for the loafers.

Charles Spurlock's Store.

Near the stove was a keg with a checker board on it, and a blue shipping crate with a piece of cardboard tacked to the top. This most important piece of furniture served as the card table where, every night, a card game broke out, called "High, Low, Jack, and the Game." There were four possible points in a single round of cards—the high card of trumps, the low card, capturing the jack of trumps, and total points, or game. The shouts and slamming of cards on the "table" were learned art forms, which I never mastered when I began to play. Over the doorway to the feed room was a giant paper wasp nest that Charlie Spurlock had found at Rock Creek Farm, and a large poster of Santa Claus holding a bottle of Coca Cola.

Above the store was the Odd Fellows Hall; the stairs to the hall had an outside entrance north of the feed room. Out back was a croquet court where players took the game very seriously, having fashioned their mallets to their own specifications, and employing strategy to win the game and infuriate their opponents. Many a time, a player having seen his ball slammed to the far reaches of the court, abruptly grabbed his mallet and went home. One year, Grandpa Songer and Arthur Jones had won the local tournament and were scheduled to play the champions from another town, but as Grandpa was sitting on the porch swing the next morning putting on his shoes, he fell dead, and a year or so later, Arthur was killed in a clay mine near Huntingburg when his pick struck an unexploded dynamite charge.

I was on Spurlock's store porch one afternoon when Ross Taylor rode up in a box wagon full of feed, pulled by a team consisting of a horse and a mule. He had been to Huntingburg and spent several hours in the taverns while waiting to have his wheat ground. As he dismounted from the wagon, he almost fell off the spring seat, then recovering his balance, tied the team to the hitching rack, and staggered onto the porch. He saw me grinning at his staggering around, pulled his pocket knife, and said: "I'll cut your ears off, you little son-of-a-bitch." I took off down the road like a shot and Ross attempted to follow me, but was in no condition to give chase. He pulled up and yelled again, "I'll remember you and the next time I see you, I'm gonna cut your ears off." Later, I saw him emerge from the store, climb up on the spring seat, and when the team pulled away with a jerk, he fell backward off the seat onto the sacks. As his rig left town, he remained that way, with his legs up on the seat. His team knew the way home and after traversing the two miles to the Taylor place in Pike County, would no doubt stop in front of the house until someone came out and helped Ross off the wagon. Back at the store, Uncle Charlie switched the plug from one side of his mouth to the other and said: "Charlie, don't mess with the Taylors. They don't make empty threats. If he could have caught you, you would have lost your ears!"

Other Duffers had run-ins with the Taylors and were careful around them, particularly when they were drinking. On one of those occasions during an all-day rain, Dorus Taylor, who had been to Huntingburg, tied his team to the hitch rail in front of Spurlock's store, stumbled in and sat by the fire, seeking to dry off. After a while, Charlie tried to get him to go home, but he hung around, being obnoxious. Leonard Weisheit was standing by the front door looking at Dorus' team of horses standing forlornly, their ears down, in the soaking rain. Leonard opined, "It's a shame to let that team stand out there in the rain like that," as he knocked his pipe out on his heel, "for anyone ought to know that's no good for a team." Dorus was in the back of the store, but somehow heard Leonard and got up and started cussing Leonard, threatening to cut him up, telling him it was none of his goddamned business. Leonard began apologizing, which had no affect on Dorus and as Dorus continued to berate him, Leonard began to cry, weeping copious tears. That seemed to touch Dorus and by that time, Charlie Spurlock had taken up for Leonard, which helped calm the situation, and at the first opportunity, Leonard fled for his life.

THE TAYLORS

I was not unaware of the Taylors and of their widely known reputation for drinking and violence. Their land abutted the Duff-Pikeville road, just across the county line in Pike County. There were three brothers—John Phil, Ben, and Theodorus, who everyone knew only as Dorus. Their father, John Taylor, had served in the Civil War, and John's father, Benjamin had come into Pike County from Kentucky and before that, the Blue Ridge Mountains. All three brothers had the lean, lanky look of eastern mountaineers.

John Phil was the leader of the clan, the heaviest drinker, and the most violent. They all farmed for a living on land bordered by the Patoka River on the north and by roads on the east and south. All their farms were within this compound and the staple crop, corn, was transformed into a more portable and potable substance, moonshine whiskey—sometimes referred to by the pioneers as "white lightnin." The sheriff of Dubois County had no jurisdiction in Pike County, and Taylor land was located a remote twenty-five miles from Petersburg, the county seat of Pike County. Besides that, no one trespassed on Taylor land. Even neighbors who were friendly with the Taylors cautioned their children never to go near certain areas. Those who lived close to them spoke highly of the Taylors as neighbors and said they were quick to lend a hand when asked. Furthermore, the Taylors respected neighbors who didn't drink. Albert McIlree, married to their sister Susan, was a religious tee-totaler, and a neighbor to the east, just inside the Dubois County line. So was Norman Stilwell, a neighbor on the west, and the Taylors abstained when helping them thresh wheat or butcher hogs. Dorus was an excellent butcher, and John Phil usually came along and spent most of his time talking to the ladies.

The Taylors were their own best friends and yet, as we will see, their own worst enemies. However, they were a sociable people. They liked to drink and play cards and often invited Duff people they knew to be drinkers to join them.

Lem and Eloise Small with baby "Sonny Boy," and Chris and wife Doris, flivvered to John Phil's log cabin one evening for a game of cards. As the evening wore on and whiskey flowed freely, everyone was having a good time until things became tense among the Taylors, and the Smalls felt it was time to leave. It had turned cold and begun snowing hard and the Model T wouldn't start, so they trekked the two miles through the deepening snow to their home just west of Duff, taking turns carrying Sonny Boy.

For a while, the Taylors sponsored dances at Dorus' home where they removed all the furniture from the large living room in the rambling frame house. They were having a merry old time one night when Beaver Taylor, John Phil's son, resented the attention being paid to his wife Pleeny, a notorious flirt, by Fuzz Kays, and pulled a knife and made for him. As Fuzz crashed through the screen door, Beaver cut a gash across Fuzz' back. Elmina, Dorus' wife, wouldn't allow dances in her home after that incident.

Plenia "Pleeny" (Stilwell), Beaver's wife, was my dad's first cousin. Dad was at Beaver's home one day, drinking with them and cutting up with Pleeny when Beaver accused him of flirting with his wife. Dad said, "Beaver, Pleeny's my own (meaning, 'first') cousin, and I'm not flirtin' with her." Beaver seemed satisfied but Dad knew it was time to leave. Generally when one of the Taylors began to get riled up, people left as quickly as possible. Years later, when Dad told me that story, I asked: "Dad, were you flirting with Pleeny?" "I guess I was," he replied. Pleeny, aware of the danger which went with living in a Taylor household, always wore a gun in her hat and if she was wearing a hat, she was wearing her gun. One Saturday evening, darkness and whiskey had overtaken Dorus and Ross (Roscoe, the son of Ben Taylor and the one I had the run-in with at Charlie's store) in Duff, and they asked Dad if they could spend the night in our barn. He readily agreed but when he obtained a blanket from the house for their use, Mom was highly displeased and never allowed the blanket to be brought back into the house. My mother, age ninety-seven as I write, has mellowed greatly since those days.

John Phil essentially raised two families. He and wife Mary (Russell) raised four children, all of whom left home, including sons Ira and James J., soon after he divorced their mother and married second wife Mary (Simpson). Before leaving home, Ira was shot twice in the stomach by William Bass when he was caught stealing watermelons from Bass. Ira was arrested for stealing and resisting arrest, and Bass for attempted murder.

Apparently, wedded bliss did not set in at the Taylor cabin because in a few short years Ella Simmons gave birth to a son Wesley, by John Phil. John Phil took the child Wesley in, and soon took in Ella as well, as his third wife. Ella was not much older than her step-sons, and when James returned home from the west, he resented Ella's presence. Their relationship went from bad to worse until James formed a murderous intent toward his stepmother. One evening, James, his father John Phil, and his cousin Ross were drinking in the town of Velpen, and James and Ross left the party early. As they passed Ross' home, James demanded that Ross obtain a "repeater" shotgun from his home. Ross asked what he wanted it for and James responded angrily, "It's none of your damn business; get it out and bring it along." From there, they went to the homes of various relatives, continuing to drink and eventually wound up at John Phil's.

On entering the house, Ross lit a lamp. Without a word, James raised the shotgun and at point blank range, shot Wesley, who was sleeping with his mother, Ella. They left the house immediately and shortly after Ella gave the alarm, Ross was arrested and jailed while James remained at large. He hid in a cave on his father's property and stayed there until hunger drove him out and he went to Dorus' home. Finding no one there, he raided the pantry and ate some food, at the same time filling his pockets. Next day, the sheriff and his posse, all heavily armed, found him hiding in John Phil's barn. He was still

Cave where James Taylor hid.

armed with the shotgun and half a quart of whiskey, but surrendered without resistance. "Poor little Wesley," he sobbed, "I would never have harmed him if I had known what I was doing. It was the whiskey, not me, that was walking around that night." At the coroner's inquest, he showed great remorse, cried like a baby and talked incoherently. He told about participating in drinking four quarts of whiskey, which they procured in Velpen, and of walking to Dorus' home, then to John Phil's, and watching Wesley and sister Mary sliding down a hill on a sled. From there, they started toward Albert McIlree's, and then he claimed he didn't remember anything. He finished his statement saying, "If I had aimed to kill anyone, it would have been my step-mother." (For no particular reason, Ella and son Wesley had changed sides in the bed that night, and when Ella saw the lamp lit and James with a gun, she pulled the featherbed over her head.)

A Pike County jury considered the evidence for twenty minutes and returned a verdict of guilty. James Taylor was sentenced to life in prison. Thirty years passed, and one Charles Aaron Proctor was arrested in California for drunk driving. From his fingerprints, the FBI determined that Proctor was one and the same person as James Taylor, who had escaped from the Indiana State prison twenty-three years earlier. Governor Schricker of Indiana sought extradition, but the governor of California refused on the grounds that Taylor had led an exemplary life for the last twenty-three years, having married and raised two step-children. Besides that, California officials indicated they believed Taylor's statement in which he said: "My step-brother (actually his half brother) was killed while I was handling a shotgun. My step-mother blamed it on me and I took the rap." This sounds like a lawyer-drafted statement, because it was literally true: Wesley was shot while James was handling the shotgun, his step-mother did blame him for Wesley's death, because she saw him shoot Wesley, and he did take the rap.

But the statement was far from the truth of what really happened. Furthermore, for some odd reason, Prosecutor Carpenter, who had sought the death penalty at the trial, told the governor of California that there was some evidence indicating that the shooting might have been accidental, and that a verdict of manslaughter would have served the ends of justice. It was accidental only in the sense that James intended to kill his step-mother and not his brother Wesley, and at the trial, the jury had been well instructed by the judge on the law of transferred intent, i.e., if you intend to kill a person, and kill someone else, it still is murder. Governor Shricker of Indiana, when informed of the decision to deny extradition, said, "That's up to California officials. If they want to keep him, they can have him." James Taylor spent the remainder of his life living in California, a free man. (Ross Taylor, shortly after the trial of James, pleaded guilty to a charge of voluntary manslaughter in the Dubois Circuit Court, where the case had been venued, and was sentenced to a term from two to twenty-one years.)

On December 10, 1933, Beaver Taylor, age forty-four, was shot to death in the Taylor cabin, which he shared with his wife Pleeny and his father, John Phil. Earlier that evening, Beaver and Louis Stillwell, Pleeny's brother, went to Duff and obtained a half-gallon of whiskey. Upon their return, the four of them drank whiskey and played cards. Louis and Beaver were partners, and Pleeny and her father-in-law John Phil, likewise. About 1:00 am, Pleeny grew tired, quit the game, and lay down in her bed in a small room off the main room of the cabin. About a half hour later, the others quit and Beaver came into the bedroom and sat down on the bed next to his wife. According to Pleeny's statement, Louis had gone to the other bedroom, but Louis, in his statement, said that he was standing next to Beaver when he was shot.

Suddenly, a handgun was pointed around the corner of the doorway that connected the two rooms and fired a bullet into the heart of Beaver Taylor, who fell from the bed to the floor, and died within five minutes. Within seconds after the first shot, two more shots were fired from outside into the cabin, one bullet passing through the outside door, and the other passing through a window pane and

John Phil Taylor's cabin as it looks today.

lodging in the wall in the kitchen. In her statement, Pleeny said: "I didn't see John Phil do the shooting but saw him in the kitchen where we had been playing cards immediately following the shooting. I did not see him have a gun."

Pleeny and her brother Louis walked to the home of a neighbor, Leo Dearing, and told him that John Phil had shot his son Beaver and asked him to go where the body lay. Leo didn't leave right away, and within five minutes, John Phil appeared on the road in front of Leo's house and said that he thought that someone had been hurt at his home and asked Leo to accompany him there. Instead, Leo agreed to go with him to the home of John Phil's sister, Susan McIlree. While they were on the way, John Phil showed him a gun and said, "He called me a coward and I shot him."

John Phil added that he had fired one shot through the window intending to shoot the "bitch or son-of-a-bitch," he wasn't sure which. John Phil claimed the others got him to playing cards and got him drunk, and he also told Leo that there had been some trouble between him and Beaver over the division of a corn crop. Then, accompanied by Robert Baldwin and Albert McIlree, both of whom were brothers-in-law of John Phil, Leo went to the Taylor cabin and found Beaver lying on his back in the doorway between the kitchen and the bed-room. "He was quite dead when we arrived about 4:00 am." After leaving the Taylor residence, he walked back to the McIlree residence, borrowed a car from Everette McIlree and drove to Pikeville where he telephoned the coroner at Petersburg. That same day, the three survivors of the card game were arrested and jailed, and a grand jury met and returned an indictment against John Phil only, and Pleeny and her brother Louis were freed.

John Phil's son Ira, who had left home many years before when he was fourteen, and who was by now a high-ranking law enforcement official from Massachusetts, and John Phil's daughter Mary from St. Louis, came for the funeral of Beaver and then visited their father in jail. They remained until after the grand jury met and then returned to their respective homes. At the trial, which was held the following

May, John Phil was represented by Ely and Corn, Petersburg attorneys. Ira and Mary returned to be at the side of their father, rendering all the help they could. Leo Dearing testified as above, and also stated under oath that John Phil told him he had used a .38 revolver, the same caliber that killed Beaver. No gun was ever found. John Phil testified on his own behalf and denied he had shot his son Beaver, denied having made the incriminating statements to Leo Dearing, saying, "I did not shoot my son—if I did I do not know it. I hadn't owned a revolver in more than twenty years. I am almost seventy-one years old. Beaver and his wife lived in part of my house. We had no trouble during the night." Pleeny testified consistently with her pretrial statement, but Attorney Corn conducted a rigorous cross-examination, which went somewhat as follows:

Q. Your name is Whitman, I believe.

A. Yes Sir.

Q. When did your name become Whitman?

A. In March.

Q. You were married to the deceased, Beaver Taylor, in December, were you not?

A. Yes Sir.

Q. Now, Mrs. Whitman, [he seemed to spit the word out], you were present on the night of December 10th when Beaver Taylor was shot?

A. Yes Sir.

Q. Isn't it a fact, Mrs. Whitman, that you awakened the defendant, John Phil Taylor, earlier that evening, to play a fourth hand at cards?

A. Yes Sir.

Q. Isn't it also a fact, Mrs. Whitman, that your brother, Louis Stilwell, and the deceased went to Duff that evening and procured the half gallon of whiskey that all of you drank during the card game?

A. Yes Sir.

Q. Now Mrs. Whitman, did you see the defendant with a gun at any time that evening?

A. No Sir.

Q. And you did not see the defendant shoot Beaver Taylor, did you?

A. No Sir.

Q. Thank you, that will be all, Mrs. Whitman.

The jury, after deliberating about an hour, reached a verdict of not guilty, and John Phil Taylor, prisoner in the Pike County jail for the last four months, was set free. As the Pike County newspaper said: "The question still is: Who shot Beaver Taylor through the heart? The full facts about it may never be known."

Many years later, Everette McIlree moved back to this area and he and I became reacquainted. We began talking about the Beaver Taylor murder and Everette took me to the Taylor cabin, which was still standing in the middle of what was then a wilderness area. He pointed out where the card game took place, the bedroom where Pleeny lay and Beaver was shot, and where the handgun came around the corner of the doorway. He told me that the sheriff had threatened to arrest him the evening of the murder for aiding and abetting John Phil by hiding the handgun. Everette said that when he saw John Phil with the handgun, he told him he had better get rid of it. "Everette," I asked, "what happened to the handgun—did you hide it?" Everette looked at me and then as if he wanted to unburden himself of something he had kept secret all these years, he said with a far away look in his eyes: "When I told John Phil he had better get rid of the gun, John Phil thought for a moment and then handed it over and asked me to hide it for him. As we walked from our residence to the Taylor cabin on the night of the murder, I lagged behind the others and hid the revolver along the road." He seemed relieved at having released himself from this painful secret and a few minutes later, showed me the place under the roots of a tree where he had stashed the weapon. Had these facts emerged at the trial, would John Phil have been convicted? What do you think?

After the acquittal, John Phil went to live with his son Ira in Massachusetts for a while, but the lure of his old haunts along the Patoka river beckoned him, and soon he returned to the area, spending his last days in Velpen.

His brother Dorus died on a bitter cold winter evening, and his body was laid on the front porch to await the coming of dawn and a trip to Pikeville by family members to summon the undertaker. When the undertaker arrived in his passenger automobile, he was unable to get Dorus' body inside the car due to the cold temperature and rigor mortis, so he departed with Dorus' legs sticking out the window. Young Ray Stilwell saw him pull away and had nightmares for a while over that scene.

What was it about the Taylors and drinking? It is too simple to say they were all alcoholics. They seemed to raise drinking whiskey to a different level—almost a spiritual one. They never went to church or talked about God or the hereafter, to anyone's recollection. At John Phil's gravesite, as he was being interred next to the graves of his murdered sons, Wesley and Beaver, several bottles of whiskey suddenly appeared in the hands of the brothers who were present. They took a long swig from the bottles they were holding, poured some onto the casket in the open grave, and then threw the still partially filled bottles into the grave to spend eternity with John Phil Taylor.

LIFE ON THE HOME FRONT

I was playing in the yard early one December morning when suddenly Mom poked her head out the door and shouted, "The Japs have bombed Pearl Harbor." I could tell from her voice that it was serious, but I wasn't sure where Pearl Harbor was. The next day at school, Miss Arensman pulled down the large world map over the blackboard and pointed out the location of Pearl Harbor. We were not unaware that trouble was brewing in that part of the world. Six Duff boys had been given draft notices and a couple of them had left for training. Don Peach had his number drawn from a goldfish bowl and left in February of 1945 for training in Georgia with the 38th Division, the Indiana National Guard. During maneuvers, anticipating a war against Germany, which was almost a year away, they trained against men dressed in German uniforms, but that was before Pearl Harbor and Don never saw Europe. He fought in the Pacific, surviving a bullet through the chest in a fight over Manila's water supply. Guthrie Sunderman began his part in the war when he went ashore at Omaha Beach, and ten days later, wrote his mother Alice, responding to her worries with good old Hard Shell Baptist doctrine of predestination and preordination she had taught him over the years:

> *The letter I got said that you hadn't heard from me for a couple of days. The reason I didn't write was because I couldn't. I know you are wondering since you know the invasion is going on, but there isn't any use in worrying as what is to be will be. That's what you always said.*

Rationing began, and Dad was always concerned about running

the car (by this time we had an old Willis-Knight) on bald tires and obtaining enough gasoline to get to his job. When we traveled by car and went downhill, Dad turned off the engine and coasted to save gasoline. Mom wondered where she would get enough sugar for canning, but Ed Ermert bought sugar on the black market and sold us what he didn't need. We kids got into the war effort to make money and to help win the war by scouring the country side for scrap iron and old wire fencing, picking milk weed pods containing a fluffy material used to stuff life jackets, and digging May Apple roots. After processing, the extract from the roots was used for medicinal purposes. A good price was offered for the roots, and I was expecting a large payday when I plunked down a large sack weighing fifty pounds or more. "Ah, but you have to let them dry, you see, at least five days in full sun." So I carried them back home and spread them on the roof of the chicken house to dry. When I sacked them up again, they weighed only a fraction of their former weight and the payday was meager.

It was announced that every community, including Duff, required a Civil Defense director. No one wanted such a ridiculous job, so I got it by default. The main reason I wanted to be Civil Defense director was that if called upon to perform official duties, I was allowed to wear a red, white, and blue arm band with the letters C D on it. It made me feel important and an integral part of the war effort. Months, even years passed, and I was never called upon to perform any official duties, that is, until 1943, when it was announced that we were to have a national blackout. I was going to get to wear my arm band and act official at last. At the given hour, if you were driving, you were to pull to the side and turn off your lights. If you were at home, you were to turn off your lights or pull your shades or curtains. As far as I could tell when I walked around Duff, everyone complied, although light from their kerosene lamps shown so faintly through the windows that it was difficult to tell.

I was pleased and proud of the cooperation of the Duffers until my last stop before returning home, which was the abode of Ed Ermert. I knocked on the door and when Ed answered, I reminded him of the blackout. He was aware of it all right and roared: "That's the dumbest goddam thing I ever heard of—tell me Charlie, how likely do you think it is that Duff will be bombed?" I agreed that Duff was probably not high on the list of strategic targets in view of the fact that the clay mine was our only industry, and it was underground. I explained that the purpose of the national blackout as it was explained to me, was to have everyone in the country doing the same thing at the same time—just part of mobilizing the people for the war effort. But Ed thought this was a lot of foolishness. It was the same attitude that caused him to take time to go to the polls at Duff School every election day only to write the word "Bullshit" across his ballot and leave.

Much of the discussion among the old men and young boys on the store porch concerned the whereabouts of Duff boys in the service. After training, they came home on leave and regaled us with stories about their experiences, new friendships they had formed, about encountering rattlesnakes and scorpions during training, about sergeants that were meaner than junk yard dogs, and about visiting cities that we had only heard about. In most instances, it was their first trip away from home, although a few of them had been in the CCC (Civilian Conservation Corps). After a while, the furloughs stopped as they were being shipped overseas. Passenger trains as long as freight trains, carrying troops, perhaps an entire regiment, went through Duff. At night, you could see the soldiers in the lighted cars, playing cards and smoking, and staring out of the windows into the dark, no doubt homesick and wondering about their fate.

We tried to keep track of the local boys through the letters they sent home. Jimmie Robertson was one of them. Before the war, he and his dad Jess were as close as father and son could be. They were constantly together, hunting, fishing, and trapping animals for fur along the Patoka River and its tributaries, north of Duff. In 1942, Jimmie was drafted. He trained in Louisiana and Texas to drive a tank, and was sent to Europe with the 638th Tank Destroyer

Battalion. He wrote to his dad:

Here it is November 5, 1944, and should be about time for the hunting to start. Hope you have good luck. There is plenty of hunting over here and you don' t need a license either, so they say.

I don't see why wars have to be, for all it leaves is death and destruction. These poor people are bombed out of practically everything.

Boy I bet I could get one of those black minks in a trap if I were there. By the way, Dad, you could try El Creek where I caught those two, remember?

He wrote again to his mother on November 17, 1944

All you can see is mud, mud, and more mud. I've got a swell pair of boots now so my feet have been dry for the last few days at least. Well Mom, I hope how soon the day will be when I can come home again to sit at the family circle and eat without getting dirt in my food. I must close now sending all my love to my dear little mother.

Love, Jimmie

But it was not to be. Ten days later, Jimmie Robertson was killed when his tank ran over a land mine. Jess and Rosie were devastated. Their world collapsed. Years afterward, the mere mention of Jimmie's name would cause this powerfully built, square-shouldered, gruff-talking man to break into tears. After the war, I set traps and fish nets with Jess a few times but it was not the same. No one could take the place of the son who was lost to him forever. Life involves so much loss. When the boys returned home, there were many late night conversations on the store porch, as those of us too young for the war pumped our young heroes for all the details of their experiences. We learned about Guthrie Sunderman's experiences on Omaha Beach and through France and Germany; Don Peach's fight at Zig Zag Pass in the Philippines, where he took a bullet through the chest; and Gene Brown's shrapnel wounds to the face, and his narrow escape when he jumped into a shell hole during an artillery barrage, only to find it occupied by three German soldiers. We envied them for having gone so far away and having seen so many sights. In a few short years, we were to get our chance, for nearly all the boys my age were in the service during the Korean War. One of the first to go was Bob Peach, who enlisted in the marines. We saw him off on Old #23 at the Duff depot on the first leg of a journey that was to take him into heavy action in Korea with the First Marine division. When I returned from the service three years later, Old #23 and #24 were no more, another casualty of the great war and the proliferation of automobiles.

Jimmie Robertson, WW II soldier.

LEAVING DUFF

After graduating from high school in 1948, I got a job at a small company which manufactured venetian blinds and repaired high school score boards, where I worked for the next few years. With the outbreak of the Korean war in 1950, my friends Buck and Bennie Borman and Chalkie Ermert and I knew we would soon be drafted. We decided to enlist, thereby choosing our branch of service and even influencing what we would do after we enlisted. We went to Evansville and then St. Louis in an effort to join the Navy. The Navy had all the men it needed. Then we tried the Air Force—same result. (Ben, probably on the strength of his math scores later got into the Navy.) Eventually, we settled for the Army, with the further understanding that we would attend the Army Clerical School after basic training.

Finally, the appointed day arrived. We gathered at the Duff Depot and waited for the eastbound evening train. Chattering nervously on the platform, we ended our conversation abruptly when we heard the wail of the whistle of old #23 as she blew for Steineker crossing, then saw her hove into view, rush past the factory pond and Hugo Lemond's stock yards and granary, and begin to blow again for the Duff crossing, the sounds of the whistle pulsating over the hills and valleys of the Duff community. Bell ringing, huffing, puffing, and blowing, she stopped for us. I started to board and stopped suddenly; with striking force, reality hit me between the eyes. Never again would I experience Duff in the same way—for my life, and Duff's way of life, was about to take a drastic and permanent new path. I paused, turned, took one last, long, lingering, look behind, and we were gone.

Thirty months later, I was on my way home on an aircraft carrier. We crossed the international date line on Christmas Day, so the next day was Christmas Day as well. A storm raged during the 24th and the first Christmas Day, and I was desperately seasick; neither food nor drink would stay down. I found relief under the wing of an F-80 fighter plane parked in the hangar deck, where I lay spread eagled so that I would have no sense of motion apart from that of the ship. Gradually, I began to improve and when it was announced that the ship was serving a huge Christmas dinner—turkey and dressing and the works, I felt I had improved sufficiently to eat. Furthermore, I was famished, so I found my way to the galley, obtained a tray heaped with steaming food and carried it to a waist-high table. (You ate standing up because chairs would move around in rough seas.) Suddenly, the ship hit a huge swell and all the trays, loaded with food, swept by me down the table, slid off the end, and formed a large pile of drumsticks, dressing, mashed potatoes, and cranberry sauce, all jumbled together. The horrible looking mess overwhelmed my queasy stomach and I hurried back to my place under the wing. Next day, the storm subsided and I discovered I would survive. Within a few days, we neared land—not just any land—it was the United States of America! I arose early on a fog-shrouded morning, anxious for the first glimpse of home, just as thirty months earlier, I leaned on the rail of another ship, straining for the first glimpse of Japanese soil. Suddenly a vivid red rising sun broke through the fog, and looming in front of us like a giant, golden harp, was the Golden Gate Bridge. We spent only one night in San Francisco, then on to Chicago by air, and a bus to nearby Fort Sheridan, where I spent an excruciatingly slow ten days going through the discharge process.

Finally, after New Year's, I was a civilian again, and caught a train for Vincennes, Indiana (passenger trains no longer passed through Duff, or for that matter, Dubois County). My family was to meet me at the station, and the anticipation of seeing them again was almost overwhelming during the train ride. As we entered the city of Vincennes, I was at the window, eager to see their faces. Then we were in the railroad yards, the depot platform came into view and then, through the window, I saw my brother Jim running alongside the train, taking long strides—God, how he had grown. Shortly, the train squealed to a halt and I was running into the arms of Mom and Dad, my sister Kate and her husband Bill, and of course, my brother Jim. We talked excitedly during the fifty mile drive home, where I was reunited with the rest of my family. They had kept the Christmas decorations up, so I was able to celebrate Christmas at home after all.

After a few hours, I became anxious to get to Duff and Wayne Hall's store. Dad said: "Charlie, folks know you are coming home, but they don't know exactly when. So let's fool em. I bought one of those big fake noses with a mustache and horn-rimmed glasses the other day. You wear it and we'll go to Duff where I will introduce you as Charlie Day, a visiting race horse man."

Glad to see that some things had not changed, I readily agreed. I put on the nose and glasses, Dad applied some makeup so that the color looked natural and we were on our way. Just north of Wayne Hall's store, we saw Uncle Tom walking toward us. As we neared each other, he immediately fixed a stare on the nose, and when Dad introduced me as Charlie Day, visiting race horse man, Uncle Tom shook my hand, said "I'm glad to meetcha," never taking his eyes off the nose. We entered Wayne's store and sat down next to the stove. None of the loafers said a word, except to say hello to Dad. Wayne emerged from the back room with a gallon of coal oil and his eyes fell on me. Without missing a beat, he said: "Hi Harold," took a couple of steps, realized I wasn't Harold, turned, did a slow double take, and said "Scuse me, I thought you wuz Harold," and continued waiting on his customer. Later Dad and I walked to the other store, which was now owned and operated by Kelso Hall, Wayne's son. We knocked on the door of the residence and Kelso's wife Flora answered the door. She fixed my nose with an unwavering stare, and when we asked for Kelse, she said he was in the store. We walked around the front of the store, and when we entered, Flora was standing there, having already entered by the back door. Later, we learned that she ran into the store and said to Kelse and other loafers: "There is a guy coming in here with Hugo Songer who has the biggest nose I have ever seen." But Kelse was not easily fooled. He took one look, grinned broadly and said: "Hi Charlie, welcome home."